A GIFT FOR:

..............................................................

FROM:

..............................................................

DATE:

..............................................................

# FIELDS
# *of* GRACE

## SHARING FAITH *from the* HORSE FARM

### Cara Whitney

#### with Michael Ross

Foreword by Dan Whitney,

"Larry the Cable Guy"

THOMAS NELSON®
*Since 1798*

Published in Nashville, Tennessee, by Thomas Nelson. Thomas Nelson is a registered trademark of HarperCollins Christian Publishing, Inc.

Published in association with the literary agency of WordServe Literary Group, Ltd., www.wordserveliterary.com

Photos on pages 10, 12, 25, 28, 37, 40, 44, 48, 58, 63, 70, 78, 82, 95, 110, 118, 126, 152, 157, 160, 166, 174, 178, 188, and 200 are by Erik Johnson: www.erikjohnsonphotography.com.

Photos on pages 18, 55, 88, 98, 103, 106, 123, 130, 136, 140, 147, 171, 184, 192, and 197 are used under license from Shutterstock.com.

Thomas Nelson titles may be purchased in bulk for educational, business, fund-raising, or sales promotional use. For information, please email SpecialMarkets@ThomasNelson.com.

ISBN-13: 978-1-4002-2009-0

*Printed in China*

21 22 23 24 25 WAI 10 9 8 7 6 5 4 3 2 1

# CONTENTS

# FOREWORD

By Dan Whitney ("Larry the Cable Guy")

I am so proud of my wife and the journey that has led her to this fantastic relationship she has with Jesus. I mean, it's incredible! In the Bible whenever Jesus was doing miracles, they always said the people "marveled" at what He had just done. That's exactly how I feel about my wife, Cara, every time she starts writing these books. I marvel. It's not the same marvel as she does with me when I don't take out the trash or the kinda marveling she extends my way when I don't clean up my side of the closet. Those marvels have negative connotations. But the marvel I'm talking about is a giddy happiness of unbelief of how God can work in a person's life when they give everything to Him. My faith itself has been strengthened by my wife's relationship with our awesome Savior. And that's exactly what it is if you're doing it right, a personal relationship with Jesus. He's our friend.

It's so crazy to me how God works. I grew up in the church: Wednesday-night prayer meeting, Sunday morning, Sunday evening, youth group, potluck dinners in the basement of the church. Many years of prayer, coleslaw, and hamburger hot dishes. Then I got in the entertainment business and fell faster than a fat guy getting off the couch with numb legs. (I can say that because I'm a fat guy, and when I sit on the couch my legs go numb, and then I . . . ugh . . . never mind, I digress.)

I tell this little story because it's an amazing look into how God works and how important evangelism is. I marveled at the fact that Jesus worked through my wife, which in turn made me, a backslid Christian, rededicate myself to the most important thing in this world: a personal relationship with Jesus. Now, this is my wife's book, so I don't want to get too long-winded in this foreword, but since I'm on the couch with numb legs from sitting with this computer, I'm obviously not moving for a while, so let me just say a few more things.

We live in a godless time. A time where Christian people need to step up and be bold about our faith. Not in a "Hey, buddy, you better yada yada yada" Bible-thumping kinda way, but in a loving "Hey, you're my friend, and I want you to know the hope and happiness I found in Jesus because I want you with me in heaven" kinda way. If you wanna be a real rebel in this world, stand up for Christ. That's being a world changer.

I know it's scary sometimes to share your faith, and we all want to be liked, but if you really care for people, the most loving thing you can do for that person is to introduce them to the truth and hope that is Jesus Christ. It's true freedom. Never, ever be ashamed to speak out about Jesus, because you never know whose life God can change in a quick conversation. It's about planting a seed and letting God do the rest. People are hurting in this world, and you may think they don't wanna hear you ramble about Jesus over an Arby's beef and cheddar, but just when you think it was all for naught, guess what? You'll more than likely be the one they come calling on when their life falls apart. Trust me, it happens all the time to *me*!

You don't have to be a world-popular renowned preacher or a

missionary to the Zulu nation to change a life. You know what ya need? You just need to be unashamed and bold enough to drop a little nugget of truth into someone's head. God has used (in worldly terms) some of the most timid, uninfluential people ever to turn *others* into world changers. The only way they were able to be a world changer is because *you* changed *their* world.

You gotta remember something: no matter where you work or what you do or what your lot in life is, we are all part of this awesome body of Christ. You may be just a pinky toe, but you're just as needed as the head, the eyes, and the ears. Everybody plays a part. That's how it works. Never think you're not in a position to share your hope. People need it and want it. They may not act like it, but now—especially in these times—they are looking for happiness, and that's a fact. You can not only give them happiness, but you can also give them hope, which will last forever. *Can I get an amen?!* This book my wife, Cara, wrote is just exactly about this: sharing the hope we all have in Jesus and standing up for what's true and right and giving people freedom in the true love of Christ. Be bold, be a rebel, and share what you have with others and watch the people marvel. God is good. Ugh . . . my legs!

# INTRODUCTION

## *Sharing Starts with Caring*

*"All authority in heaven and on earth has been given to me.
Therefore go and make disciples of all nations, baptizing them
in the name of the Father and of the Son and of the Holy Spirit,
and teaching them to obey everything I have commanded you.
And surely I am with you always, to the very end of the age."*
MATTHEW 28:18–20

Matthew 28 shares such encouraging words from Jesus. Yet for some of us, these verses trigger more guilt than comfort. We think, *How can I "go and make disciples of all nations" when reality forces me to stay where I am?* We have families to take care of, demanding jobs, busy schedules, and a big stack of bills to pay each month. The reasons not to "go" all sound good on paper. But honestly. Was Jesus really talking to everyday, ordinary people?

I wondered these things too. I mean, I'm a farm girl, so I'm used to multitasking—but this can feel a bit overwhelming. And before I committed my life to Christ, I thought that churches were filled with hypocrites and that most believers were, well, just plain crazy. To me, they were all ranting street-corner evangelists who waved "Turn or Burn" tracts in people's faces and then exclaimed, "Jesus loves you!" *Say what?!* They'd pound the pulpit, shake the Bible like a weapon over peoples' heads, and speak a language I didn't understand:

"The Lord separates the sheep from the goats."

"Repent."

"We're sinners who have been saved by the blood of the Lamb."

I couldn't help noticing that Christians manufactured their own lines of jewelry with crosses and purity rings, and they had their own tattoos. They posted bumper stickers on their cars claiming, "I'm not perfect, just forgiven," right next to a silver fish symbol. There were "Christians only" housing communities. Christian business owners gave discounts to those who would say "I'm a Christian" or "I work at [fill in the blank] ministry." They had their own buzzwords, such as *cell groups, megachurches, born again,* and *on fire.* The churches some attended determined their status. Many even dressed alike.

Honestly, I was confused. And maybe I'm stubborn or just a slow study, but it took years of asking questions, observing Christ-followers, and seeking the one, true God of the Bible before I could commit my life to Him. So what finally clicked for me? I eventually met Christ-followers who were 100 percent genuine. These particular folks weren't into gimmicks and sales pitches, and they didn't hide in a subculture. They truly loved God and were committed to sharing that love with everyone they met. True, some of them were weird, and none of them were perfect, yet they were authentic. They helped me realize that God forgives me and loves me exactly the way I am. I didn't have to perform or try to be someone different. I discovered that Jesus wants me to be *me.*

Eventually I clued in to a secret that would guide my relationship with God for the rest of my life: *I needed to fall in love with Jesus!* I needed to pursue Christ as my closest companion and best friend in life. It was important to put all else aside to be with Him. And it's the same today. He must be the priority of my heart, even while I attend to the everyday business of life. Being in relationship with Him isn't about religion or following the rules. To be in *true relationship* with Jesus means pursuing

I didn't have to perform or try to be someone different. I discovered that Jesus wants me to be *me*.

*His heart,*
*His passions,*
*His character,*
*His truth.*

What's more, I must be His hands, His feet, and a reflection of His love to others. Nurturing a relationship with someone involves trust, transparency, surrender, and above all, a two-way connection. Close friends—especially lovers—must talk and grow together *daily*, not just occasionally. (Makes sense, right?) It's the same with God.

Our eyes can't be fixed on "Churchianity": looking Christian, saying Christian things to impress Christian family and friends, all the while thinking it also impresses God.

If we let Him, Jesus will begin a painful work in us. It won't happen overnight—and it will come with a mix of joy, tears, and the heart-pounding expectation that our lives are taking a radical new turn. He'll slowly strip away the masks, the false assumptions, the bad theology, the idols, and the chilly layers between Him and us, and little by little our hearts will warm up to Him. And somewhere along the way, we'll discover that we just can't keep quiet about this amazing thing that has happened to us. The love we share with our Savior will overflow and touch others. Christ's love is much too great to be contained in a single human heart. It must be lived out and multiplied! "May the Lord make your love increase and overflow for each other and for everyone else, just as ours does for you" (1 Thessalonians 3:12).

> Christ's love is much too great to be contained in a single human heart.

It's this kind of relationship that has compelled me to "go!"

Behind every human life is a story, and behind every story is the Author—the Builder of history, the Maker of the ages, our loving Creator who reveals Himself through a book. The Bible is His message of salvation; the ultimate story of restoration, of hope, of eternal life through Jesus Christ. And God is calling us to take His story to heart—living it, working it out in our daily lives, and sharing it with everyone we meet.

Once I made the decision to receive Christ, I knew I was saved, but I have to admit that in the days after my conversion I didn't feel any different than before. I found myself asking, *Okay, God . . . now what?*

I desperately wanted to feel something deeper with Jesus, but how would I go about grabbing intangible faith and making it my own? I spent hours feeding a need for biblical knowledge, cramming in as much information about the "whys" as I could. I did Bible study after Bible study, seven days a week, memorizing Scripture.

Also, during this time my body started breaking down. I had lost fifteen pounds of weight, and I had no idea why. As I stood in my kitchen receiving a phone call from my doctor saying that I needed to have more tests, I glanced up at a chalkboard where I had written 1 Peter 5:7: "Cast all your anxiety on him because he cares for you."

I desperately wanted to feel something deeper with Jesus, but how would I go about grabbing intangible faith and making it my own?

Up until that moment, it was just another verse that I was trying to memorize. But as I stood there in that swaying room feeling like I just had half the breath kicked out of my chest, I suddenly became spiritually alive!

I had the realization that despite believing in Jesus, I had not gone all in yet. I had not cast everything on God. I had given Him my mind but not anything else, and I was still holding on to things I thought I could control. No matter what my health diagnosis was, what really mattered was how I glorified God through whatever purposeful journey He placed me on. It was a moment that lasted only a matter of seconds, but I can tell you that nothing but God mattered in that kitchen—not my husband, not my kids. Just Him.

It was the moment in which my life became God's completely, and I became saved with the purpose of furthering the gospel, not as a reward for all the studying I had been doing but because I was willing to give Him the most protected part of me. I gave Him my heart, and He gave me a heart for the lost.

At this very moment, there are 151,600 people in this world preparing for a tomorrow that will never come.[1] That makes me want to roll up my sleeves, because I wonder how many of them have been told about Jesus.

How many of them are spiritually dead? Each of them will exist eternally. But where will they spend it? In heaven with God or forever separated from Him? It hinges on how they responded to Jesus and His gift of salvation. Yet I can't help but wonder, *Have they been told?*

> I gave Him my heart, and He gave me a heart for the lost.

Christianity is not a rest stop on the way to heaven. If you truly believe Jesus is Savior of the world, and you believe that He will come back again for the church, then this world should not be able to keep you quiet.

Jesus told us there is joy in heaven for every sinner who comes to repentance. Let's give heaven 151,600 more reasons to rejoice today!

# CHAPTER 1

# EVANGELISM: A DIRTY WORD?

*Christ's love compels us, because we are convinced that
one died for all, and therefore all died. And he died for all,
that those who live should no longer live for themselves
but for him who died for them and was raised again.*

2 CORINTHIANS 5:14–15

When I was a farm kid in Wisconsin, I owned some beautiful horses. But the first one I purchased as an adult is a horse I still own today— and one I absolutely adore.

His name is Orlando, and he is the cover model of my first book, *Unbridled Faith*. He's a stunner with his beautiful chestnut coloring and gorgeous blond locks. Orlando is truly the "Ken doll" of horses! And he has an adorable personality to boot, drawing people in with authentic affection.

Because he's so gentle with strangers, Orlando now serves an important role as a therapy horse. For several days now, he's been out at a ranch in Hickman, Nebraska—a stone's throw from our farm near Lincoln.

Orlando is helping a young girl internally process the loss of her grandmother. He has become a patient friend to this grieving child, letting the girl brush him and lean into him. I'm so thankful that my favorite horse is being used for such a noble purpose!

But I'll be honest: I sometimes catch myself wondering how that's even possible. This beautiful creature also has a dark side.

Orlando is extremely jealous of other horses, which makes him very aggressive toward them. While I'm no horse behaviorist, I think part of the problem is that he was raised to be a dressage horse. In other words, he lived in a stall his entire life and was trained to run patterns in an arena. He was never let out into a pasture to learn the etiquette of living in a community. In a sense, he's been institutionalized his whole life, so he views other horses as competition.

> I'm so thankful that my favorite horse is being used for such a noble purpose!

I've tried on several occasions to nudge Orlando over this hump, and a couple of years ago I thought I'd found the answer. I decided to pair him up with some of my more passive horses—a herd of my four-legged friends that were, as horse folk would say, "low in the pecking order." I was sure Orlando would automatically be crowned king, and with that, he would enjoy a life of grazing peacefully with other horses.

I gave Orlando a few months to commune over the fence with the herd. When his interactions with them seemed healthy, I decided it was time to open the gate that had separated them. Big mistake.

Before I could stop him, Orlando launched an all-out barnyard brawl!

Almost immediately, he started chasing my youngest Norwegian Fjord horse, Oaken, biting at him and trying to push him down.

I sprang into action, yelling and waving my hands, desperately trying to get Oaken to run behind the gate I was holding open. I needed to separate the two 1,200-pound animals, but how? Doing so would risk getting me and Oaken killed.

As my adrenaline surged, my moment of helplessness turned into instinct. I hopped on a four-wheeler, which was attached to a manure spreader, and I told my high-school-aged helper, Lindsay, to open the main pasture gate and seek a safe place out of the way.

My plan: Try to place the poop rig between Orlando and Oaken, who by this time was about to collapse with exhaustion. If that happened, Orlando would stomp the life out of the young horse.

I zoomed full throttle through that gate with dirt, grass, and gravel flying everywhere. As I picked up speed, the manure spreader went airborne right behind me. At that very moment, right there in the heat of the battle, I began feeling like the flustered dad in the movie *A Christmas Story*. And like him, I, too, wove a tapestry of "colorful adjectives" that as far as we know is still hanging in space over Nebraska!

The spreader eventually landed, and I somehow managed to place the rig between Orlando and Oaken. Instantly, Orlando galloped full speed out of the pasture and into the yard in front of my barn. Lindsay shut the gate, and the drama was over.

> I, too, wove a tapestry of "colorful adjectives" that as far as we know is still hanging in space over Nebraska!

Once the dust settled and my heart rate returned to normal, I had to face the obvious: Orlando is a real-life Jekyll and Hyde with two contrasting personalities. And it's his Hyde personality that gets me worked up. But there was something else that I began to see clearly. I, too, have a good side and a bad side that are at war within me. (Actually, we all do.) Sometimes in the heat of battle, my own

"Hyde personality" gets the best of me. Remember the colorful adjectives? Lindsay witnessed every second of it, and that made my heart sink.

I want nothing more but to share Christ with my young friend, so the thought of reverting back to my old self when the pressure was on really shook me up. *Can God use a Jekyll-and-Hyde Christian?* I started wondering. *Do I have what it takes to mentor someone?*

The answer, of course, is *yes*! If the Lord can use a flawed horse to comfort a grieving child, He can certainly count on a flawed human to lead someone to Him. (Just open your Bible for proof!) My witness was still intact, and Lindsay and I were able to laugh about the flying manure spreader.

While I didn't like having to face my own shortcomings during Orlando's barnyard brawl, that crazy experience has helped me rethink evangelism.

For starters, I'm dropping the perfect performance approach, acting as if I have everything figured out. The Bible says, "All have sinned and fall short of the glory of God" (Romans 3:23). So I think authenticity is the answer. And I'm not turning evangelism into a big sales presentation. Instead, I'm sharing from the heart because Scripture says, "Christ's love compels us" (2 Corinthians 5:14). That, too, is the key.

Recently my husband was on Twitter and came across a man who insisted that certain individuals were going to burn in hell. "Repent or burn!" the man tweeted.

Boy, this guy made us angry. But truthfully, the individuals he was calling out were, in fact, destined for hell if they didn't get their hearts right with God. Yet I couldn't help feeling so conflicted.

While this guy spoke truth, I wanted to punch him in the mouth. I had such a hard time with his delivery of the gospel, and I had to wonder if he cared about souls or if he just wanted to let others know they weren't part of the club. And did he think he was impressing God with his boldness? I will never know the heart of another man, so I truly can't say. Thankfully, God is the Judge. While there was truth in this man's message, the messenger was so off-putting, I can't imagine how anyone would want what he claimed to have.

Is this an example of why *evangelism* is treated like a dirty word these days? I think so. Damage has been done in the name of Christ by those who lack true love of all people.

> Did he think he was impressing God with his boldness?

As we share our faith, our motivation shouldn't be to win an argument with someone or to intentionally agitate folks. And we cannot, under any circumstance, share the gospel from an attitude of spiritual pride or a position of superiority.

None of us is perfect. And my flawed but beautiful Orlando has shown me that we all have a good side and a bad side at war within us. Every one of us needs the Savior.

Let's return *evangelism* to the loving action that it should be. With authentic affection, we need to help people understand that we're all lost without God. Yet the Lord hasn't abandoned us. He loves us too much! Jesus told us, "I am the light of the world. Whoever follows me will never walk in darkness, but will have the light of life" (John 8:12).

..................................................................................................

Lord, give me the courage to share Your love with those You place in my path. Help me face my own flaws and shortcomings and witness with confidence. Let others see You in my life. Amen.

# CHAPTER 2

# PASSION, COWS, AND QUITTERS

*We are careful not to judge people by what they seem to be, though we once judged Christ in that way. Anyone who belongs to Christ is a new person. The past is forgotten, and everything is new. God has done it all! He sent Christ to make peace between himself and us, and he has given us the work of making peace between himself and others.*

2 CORINTHIANS 5:16–18 CEV

I loved growing up on my family's cattle farm in northern Wisconsin. For the first nineteen years of my life, that *was* my life—my whole world. I cherish each memory of that special place—especially the people and the experiences that shaped me into the rough-and-tumble country girl I am today. And though I didn't know it at the time, farm life prepared me for motherhood!

Each spring my family would calve around four hundred head of Black Angus babies, and it was my job to take care of each one of them. Imagine tending to the bellowing, bleating cries of so many little ones.

Each morning I'd pack two sandwiches in my saddle bag and head into the endless acres of rolling pastures. Around lunchtime I'd eat one sandwich, and then I'd give the second to my horse, Roanie. Man, I loved that animal! We were best friends, spending our summers riding among the herd of cattle without a care in the world. With each of Roanie's steps, I'd hear the soft creak of saddle leather, the occasional chirp of a chestnut-sided warbler in the distance, the low mooing of the cattle all around me.

These are by far my favorite childhood memories. The years I spent riding through Wisconsin pastureland are a season of my life that, no matter how hard I try, I'll never be able to relive. That season is gone. But I can still hope that since the Bible talks about the pearly gates on the new earth, maybe those gates are actually there to keep the cows in. And maybe I'll get to ride again among them!

So you can picture how excited I was when my daughter, Reagan, who at the time was five, became horse obsessed and asked to take riding lessons. Granted, there weren't any cows in the picture, but horses would do. I enthusiastically signed her up. But as the weather got colder and the demands grew harder, she slowly started losing interest in riding. Her passion for horses was short-lived.

> I can still hope that since the Bible talks about the pearly gates on the new earth, maybe those gates are actually there to keep the cows in.

Fast-forward six years, and my now-eleven-year-old daughter who, at this point, has tried (and quit) every activity she has ever shown interest in tells me she'd like to dance. *Really—dance?!*

I don't know much about dancing, but because I never want my kid to tell her friends later in life that her parents didn't allow her to follow her dreams, Dan and I reluctantly signed her up. We expected that given her track record, she would most likely quit. I said to a close friend, "This whole thing is so unorganized. Are these girls learning anything about dance, or is this studio just taking our money?"

Okay, I admit it. I was secretly trying to sabotage my daughter's dance aspirations. But since she was a serial quitter, I figured we might as well get this quitting business over with.

This time I was wrong.

Much to my surprise, our daughter has stuck with it.

On recital night the house lights went down at the Lied Center in Lincoln, Nebraska, and the curtain went up. And you know what? The experience was absolutely incredible! My mind was blown, and the rest of me was humbled. In that moment I was met with the realization that I am a total knucklehead. I leaned over to my friend Tracy and said, "This is the moment in which I'm convinced that I should not talk about things I really know nothing about."

I am learning about dance, and honestly, I'm becoming really excited about it. My daughter's passion is contagious!

I can only imagine what my family must have thought when I suddenly became passionate for Jesus Christ. I was a former quitter myself and a known liar. I was the person who made several bad choices. I completely understand why the people who knew me at my worst had a hard time accepting me as a "new creation."

The great example of a changed life is Saul of Tarsus, who the Christian church considered "public enemy number one." He seemed to go along easily with the stoning of Stephen. So when Ananias was asked to help Saul, he naturally found it hard to comprehend. Saul then went to Jerusalem to try and join up with the disciples, and they reacted like any of us would: they were afraid of him. *Gosh, I don't know, Saul. We need to have a group meeting about this.*

It's hard to be labeled as the person you were in the past. It's even harder once you've made a radical change. After I committed my life to Christ, I began working hard to grow in my faith. But I'll never forget the reaction of a family member who nonchalantly said to me, "You're a selfish person, and you've always been that way. That's just who you are."

Hearing this was so hurtful because that's simply not who I am anymore. God made me, and He is continuing to remake me. The day I became a Christ-follower and invited Jesus to clean up my spiritual life is the day I began the really hard part of my journey. Remaking me is something God is still doing, something He'll continue doing for the rest of my life.

True, I still have a lot more to learn—certainly about dancing, and probably much more about motherhood. (Human kids are much more complex than calves!)

But there's one thing I'm convinced of: I think it's time to step over the person I used to be. Anyone who belongs to Christ is a new person. "The past is forgotten, and everything is new." That's the hope I need to share.

Lord, while I cannot change my past, I can use it to change the future of the people around me. Please let others see the change in me. My prayer is that You will become contagious to those who see You in my life. Amen.

# CHAPTER 3

# BY ADDING YOU'RE SUBTRACTING

*Do not add to what I command you and do*
*not subtract from it, but keep the commands*
*of the LORD your God that I give you.*
DEUTERONOMY 4:2

For a kid who adored farm life and animals, there was no better job for my personality than bottle-feeding baby calves over the summer. Beginning each March, our cattle would start having babies. This time period was known as calving season, which was always a stressful time for my parents, who depended on our family's cattle operation to put food on the table and pay the bills. My parents' biggest obstacle by far was the unpredictable springtime Wisconsin weather. It can be warm one day, and a blizzard can blow across the fields the next. So the cows (especially the first-time mothers) would have to be checked around the clock so newborn babies wouldn't freeze to death. Calves were weighed, tagged, and checked to make sure they had been up and had nursed to get their mothers' first milk full of all those life-saving antibodies.

If a cow had twins, or we encountered the occasional cow that would shirk her parental responsibilities, we would take the calf away and I would bottle-feed it. Sometimes a calf is left without the care of its mom. The best thing to do is to take it and pair it with another cow that has lost a calf. Placing these newborn calves in the orphan pen gives them the opportunity to be cared for during their early years. That was my job.

> Placing these newborn calves in the orphan pen gives them the opportunity to be cared for during their early years.

I would have a revolving door of little ones until the end of May, adding and subtracting bottle calves until whoever was left over would be mine to love and take care of for the rest of the summer. I would feed them, brush them, lead them around, and take naps with them under my great-grandma Connie's crab apple tree. I did this until the fall leaves turned colors and dropped to the ground. At that point, it was time to head back to school. With tears streaming, I would say goodbye to my friends, and they would be sent off to the feedlot. At a young age, I learned the powerful life lesson of letting go, especially when it's for a good reason.

Months later, spring would burst back into action and the calving cycle would start over.

Life is a little like my orphan pen. We are constantly adding and subtracting and making decisions. People come in and go out; we change jobs; our kids change before our eyes. Toddlers become teens in the blink of an eye, and then they become adults and are out the door.

Dan and I always found it easiest when we were able to make all the decisions for our kids—what they should eat, what they should wear, where they should go. Parenting gets harder as they become old enough to make their own choices. And here's one of the hardest things of all: watching your kids live out the consequences of their decisions.

Jesus said, "I am the way and the truth and the life. No one comes to the Father except through me" (John 14:6). The Lord deserves our eternal praises for that truth, and He gives us a clear choice: either we follow Him or we don't. We have to pick from just two doors, and before we choose, He lets us know what is on the other side of each of them. Door number one, His door, leads to everlasting life, while option two leads to destruction.

You'd think that we'd all go for door number one. But sadly, that is not the case, and there are people out there who would rather choose destruction. When people ask, "If God is so good, why does He send people to hell?"—the truth is, they choose to go there themselves. If they don't want anything to do with God in this life, why would we expect them to want to be in His presence forever? Still, it's painful watching people stumble through this life without God.

He gives us a clear choice: either we follow Him or we don't.

Maybe that's why some well-meaning believers try to sweeten the deal by adding other options: "Well, as long as you stay positive and are nice to others, God will consider that. And what is hell anyway? Maybe it's a bad emotion or a negative thought."

Some try to soften the language of the Bible because they desperately want people to choose the right door. Yet the Bible makes it clear that we cannot add to or subtract anything from God's Word. Why? Because we could risk taking away from the point. And by adding, we're subtracting what Jesus did on the cross.

Here's what Revelation 22:18–19 tells us:

> I warn everyone who hears the words of the prophecy of this scroll: If anyone adds anything to them, God will add to that person the plagues described in this scroll. And if anyone takes words away from this scroll of prophecy, God will take away from that person any share in the tree of life and in the Holy City, which are described in this scroll.

I don't know much about the "begots" and the "cubits" and things like that in the Bible, but I do know what Jesus says. There is one gospel and nothing more. No one can come to God the Father except through the Son, Jesus Christ (John 14:6).

An effective witness for Christ gives others the tools to make the choice between the two doors. They may choose door number two, but that's not up to us. Our job is to love people so much, they encounter the truth through our words and deeds (Colossians 3:17). God is the One who will knock on the doors of their hearts and add to His kingdom.

> I don't know much about the "begots" and the "cubits" and things like that in the Bible, but I do know what Jesus says. There is one gospel and nothing more.

...........................................................................

Lord, thank You for the privilege of serving You and sharing the gospel. Guide my tongue and my steps. Help me lead others to the truth through my words and actions. Amen.

# CHAPTER 4

# HIDING FROM THE SCHWAN'S MAN

*"Listen! I am standing at the door, knocking; if you*
*hear my voice and open the door, I will come in*
*to you and eat with you, and you with me."*
REVELATION 3:20 NRSV

T he persistent knocking on our front door had finally stopped, yet my mom wasn't taking any chances. She pressed a finger to her lips, signaling my younger sister and me to remain perfectly still. I just nodded and played invisible by the refrigerator, pretending I was a ninja.

But for an antsy, talkative twelve-year-old, remaining perfectly still was torture. I wanted to be outside having adventures with my favorite horse, Roanie. Instead, we were wasting daylight, holing up in the kitchen like fugitives from the law.

I glanced at the clock on the microwave and groaned. *It has been only fifty-nine seconds? I don't care. It's time for action!*

I winked at my sister, and then inch by inch—and without making a peep—I stealthily slid along the wall and made it to the kitchen door. I froze and just listened for a second.

*Silence.*

Then I rolled my head around the corner and peeked into the living room with one eye.

*All clear.*

I tiptoed toward our front window. The man standing on our porch was gone, including the bright yellow truck he showed up in. (Little did I know, the truck was parked in a different spot.) "Come out, come out wherever you are," I blurted playfully.

"Shush!" my mom gasped, emerging from the kitchen and waving her arms. Suddenly, the knocking started again.

*What?!* I panicked, and when I turned around I saw the guy squinting through the window. My eyes zeroed in on his red shirt with the familiar swan embroidered on it. I instantly raced back into the kitchen and took my post by the refrigerator.

> "Shush!" my mom gasped, emerging from the kitchen and waving her arms.

"Why can't we just answer the door?" I pleaded.

"Quiet, Cara!"

"Bet he has the ice cream we like," I said, "and I really want some."

My sister chimed in, "I'll take chocolate chip cookie dough and fudge ripple—"

"We're not buying ice cream," Mom interrupted. "Now please be still!"

"Why not? And why do we always hide from this guy?"

"Shush!"

It was summer on the farm, sometime in the mid-1980s, and I was experiencing another weird but fairly common family quirk: hiding from the Schwan's man . . . and just about every other salesperson who came knocking.

As the weather warmed up, door-to-door venders roamed the back-roads of our little neck of the woods, hawking everything from vacuum cleaners to Bibles. And they often found themselves on our doorstep, *always* at the worst possible moment.

We'd hear a *tap, tap, tap* on our front door, and if we suspected it was a salesperson, my mom would shoo us into the kitchen to hide. Now, before you jump to conclusions about her, let me explain something. No, she didn't suffer from anthropophobia (fear of people, or salespeople for that matter), and she wasn't in the witness protection program (yet I admit my curiosity often got the best of me with that last thought).

The truth is, Mom was just too kind to turn people away.

Except for the Fuller Brush man—who she'd never hide from. I think it was because this guy was so old and so sweet, and he didn't seem to have much money—or at least that was his angle. He'd drop by only a couple of times a year, opening his big suit-

> The truth is, Mom was just too kind to turn people away.

case full of brushes. Mom would feign interest as he gave his spiel, and then she'd dig into her purse and pull out enough loose dollar bills and change to buy a hairbrush from him.

Her heart was always in the right place.

As for the other door-to-door venders, we didn't have anything against them, especially the Schwan's folks. (We loved their ice cream—and still do to this day!) It's just that my mom had limited time, so it was easier to hide in the kitchen.

Many years later, after I got married and started my own family in Nebraska, a very special person started knocking on my door. He was far from a salesman, and what this guy offered was free—and worth so much more than anything in the world. I'm talking, of course, about Jesus.

Looking back, I now see that He had been standing at the door of my heart for many years, persistently knocking, patiently waiting. But time and time again I hid, making plenty of excuses about why I couldn't invite Him in.

One day as I was folding laundry, I found a card in my husband's pocket with a prayer of salvation printed on it. Even though I was not yet a believer, I felt compelled to save the prayer. Later I learned that Dan had received it from a couple he had dinner with in Las Vegas—Stryper guitarist Oz Fox and his wife, Annie Lobert. Annie had been a prostitute for sixteen years until a drug overdose nearly ended her life. After she recovered and received a second chance, Annie committed her life to Jesus. Soon, she sensed a tug in her heart to minister to girls and women who were trapped in prostitution.

> Annie had been a prostitute for sixteen years until a drug overdose nearly ended her life.

In 2007, Annie launched a ministry called Hookers for Jesus, which is committed to reaching—and ultimately rescuing—women who are victims of sex trafficking. Since Annie knows what to look for and where to look, she can easily identify them. She gives them resources, connection, relationship, and a way out. And she tells victims they are valuable and deeply loved by God.

Annie's story touched my heart. Dan shared it with me, along with details of that very special dinner meeting he had with Annie and Oz. We were both so amazed by this couple's radical transformation. Still, it would take several more months before I was ready for a heart change. (Remember all those excuses I mentioned earlier?)

But eventually it happened.

I began to see so clearly that the Lord is patient and good and that He doesn't want anyone to be lost (2 Peter 3:9). One day the persistent knocking on the door of my own heart grew louder, and I had run out of excuses—and places to hide. So I raced upstairs to my nightstand where I kept the card from Annie's ministry. I flipped it over and began to recite the prayer:

> Dear God, I know that I am a sinner. I believe that Jesus Christ, Your Son, died on the cross for my sin and rose from the dead to be my Lord. God, I now repent of my sin and personally invite Jesus into my life. Thank You, Jesus, for giving me the free gift of eternal life. I promise to live for You as You reveal Yourself to me through Your Word, the Bible. In Jesus' name I pray. Amen.

I had finally opened the door and invited Jesus in.

While I've never met Annie, I'm pretty sure she'd be tickled to hear that one of her cards made it off the streets where she intended it to be and traveled all the way to Nebraska.

The prayer on the back found its way into the quiet laundry room of a housewife who was curious about Christ.

I truly believe God is working to bring sinners home—so much that I started leaving business cards with John 3:16 printed on them and an

> The prayer on the back found its way into the quiet laundry room of a housewife who was curious about Christ.

e-mail address people can contact us to get a free Bible. I place them at restaurants and offices with the hope that maybe just one person who has been thinking about Jesus would save a card in their pocket, waiting for the day when they are ready to invite Christ in.

People may seem as if they are not paying attention when we are speaking to them about our faith, but they are. A lot of times they are watching us from the kitchen until that moment when their need for more than ice cream hits and they open the door.

God is orchestrating the salvation plan of every man, woman, and child; and as we share our faith, we're actually partnering with Him. (Let that soak in!)

Here's the best thing we can do: trust that God is at work through our efforts. Without His hand, how else could a former prostitute in Las Vegas minister to a housewife in Nebraska?

........................................................................................

Lord, Jesus, thank You for never giving up on me. You've persistently knocked at the door of my heart, and You've patiently waited for me to respond. Use me to touch the world with Your goodness. Help me never to miss an opportunity to share the gospel. Amen.

# CHAPTER 5

# ELECTRIC BIBLE THUMPERS

*My dear friends, with our tongues we speak both praises
and curses. We praise our Lord and Father, and we curse
people who were created to be like God, and this isn't right.*

JAMES 3:9–10 CEV

Not long ago, as I was walking through a pasture and making the rounds on our farm, I noticed a wire popping out of an insulator on our electric fence. I eyed the thing for a second, dreading the inevitable. *Yep—that needs immediate attention*, I told myself. Task one million and one . . . and yet the day had only just begun!

Since an insulator is made of glass or plastic, it not only holds the wire in place, it keeps it from touching something that could ground the electricity and render the fence useless. Insulators ensure that the electrically charged wires deliver their memorable zaps—keeping predators out and farm animals in.

While I'm not a huge fan of electric fences, I know that without them my feisty horses would push down the barrier and wander into crops that might give them colic. I had to keep them safe, so I had to fix that fence. The first order of business was to shut off the power. The second, reattach the wire to the insulator. That was the part I dreaded most. It meant that I'd actually have to touch the wire. *Ugh!*

If you've ever had a bad experience with electricity—whether it was a jolt from a fence or a zap from an outlet—I'm sure you can relate to my squeamishness. Logic assured me that the power was off and everything was safe, but fear got the best of me. Each time I reached my hand toward the wire, I simply could not latch onto it.

> Each time I reached my hand toward the wire, I simply could not latch onto it.

Scenes from *Jurassic Park* flooded my brain. I imagined the professor and the kids dangling from the giant dinosaur-proof fence just as the power kicked on and 100,000 volts of death surged toward them.

I must have checked the indicator light on the electric box at least three times before I mustered up enough courage to grab the wire. Eventually I made contact, fixed the problem without a single jolt, and moved on to daily farm task one million and two!

Getting zapped by electricity sends pain and fear through us that's hard to shake. Insensitive words that enter our ears aren't easily forgotten either.

This whole fence ordeal made me think a lot about that. When I was a new Christian, one of the things that really terrified me was the thought of walking into a church and interacting with other believers. Sometimes their words weren't very kind. And sometimes I didn't feel very loved or accepted by them. It felt a lot like a painful jolt. I was even afraid that if I hung around them long enough, I'd begin to act just like the ornery, electric Bible thumpers who had hurt me in the past.

I'll never forget some harsh words I received from a Christian co-worker nearly twenty years ago. One day I asked him if I could attend his church. His response caught me off guard: "No," he said, "since you're not a member of our denomination, I don't think you'll be welcome there."

*What? Not welcome! Doesn't God welcome everyone?*

At the time, I had zero background in theology, so I couldn't help feeling confused, angry, and deeply devastated. I even started to doubt myself, fearing that I'd missed the opportunity to know God. *Maybe I'm too lost to be a Christ-follower,* I concluded. *Maybe I was created for evil.*

Those are crazy thoughts that are far from the truth, right? Yet I felt like an outsider being zapped by a big electric fence around the church.

> I felt like an outsider being zapped by a big electric fence around the church.

Eventually I learned how the Lord really feels about me (and you):

> I am convinced that neither death nor life, neither angels nor demons, neither the present nor the future, nor any powers, neither height nor depth, nor anything else in all creation, will be able to separate us from the love of God that is in Christ Jesus our Lord. (Romans 8:38–39)

Still, there was no way I was going to walk into a church. I was afraid of being zapped again, afraid I'd end up feeling the way I was made to feel about myself in the past. And I just didn't want to deal with that kind of negativity.

I remember the day the Holy Spirit laid on my heart that I needed to find other believers to help me grow. Soon, a dear friend named Ann invited me on a playdate with her and her son. Our boys became preschool buddies, and so our lives became intertwined forever. (Just how deeply we became intertwined, I will divulge later in this book.) And I've never asked Ann this, but I wonder what the expression was on my face when she reached out with her first invite to church. Terror maybe? I remember thinking the "old me," before Christ, would have made up a lie on the spot, that we were going out of town or something. But I agreed, and I am so glad I did. Ann was my first Christian friend.

Ann did it up right. She asked me to coffee, and she facilitated multiple playdates. She didn't know where I was spiritually, but she cared about me. Contrary to how some interpret Matthew 18:20, "two or three" doesn't make a church, but it is a great place to start helping someone on their spiritual journey.

As I grew in my faith, the Holy Spirit nudged me through the threshold of those double doors, and I found my place among the body of believers.

While some Christians behave like electric Bible thumpers, spewing words that are far from kind, and others put barriers between themselves and those outside the church, the truth is, we're all broken and need Jesus. You, me, my friend Ann . . . even the Bible thumpers. And as Ann taught me, it's not our job to fix anyone. If we say we trust God, then we must also trust that He will do the fixing. It is our job to listen, love, and care—and let Christ do the rest.

.....................................................................................

Lord, help me not be jaded by all the painful zaps I have received from others. Teach me how to be patient and loving— both with Christians and those who aren't yet believers. And show me how to tame my tongue and share words that heal. Amen.

CHAPTER 6

# RETHINKING CRAZY MOTIVES

*"You study the Scriptures diligently because you think that in them you have eternal life. These are the very Scriptures that testify about me, yet you refuse to come to me to have life."*
JOHN 5:39–40

The other day a friend told me a crazy true story about his mother-in-law's mixed-up priorities. As he and his family were buzzing down the road, heading to church one Sunday morning, he noticed a stranded motorist. As he got closer, he could see a well-dressed older woman standing next to a car. She was holding a Bible in one hand and her purse in the other. She looked a bit dazed and confused—just staring dumbfoundedly at her front left tire, which was as flat as a pancake.

Just as my friend slowed down to pull over, his mother-in-law leaned forward from the back seat and grabbed his shoulder. "Don't you even think about stopping," she blurted. "You'll make us late for church!"

While my friend and I groaned at the absurdity of that moment, I couldn't help thinking how his story describes the self-centered motives of way too many believers. We waste our time and energy checking off religious boxes and end up missing opportunities to live our faith. It seems we'd rather *play church* than *be the church*.

"You're in my prayers," we tell others . . . but then we forget to pray.

> It seems we'd rather *play church* than *be the church*.

"I'll stop by and visit the shut-ins," we promise . . . but then we run out of time.

"Yes, I'll help out in children's church," we boldly profess . . . but then we spend the next six months hiding from the children's pastor.

Before I committed my life to Christ, my husband, Dan, and I decided to put our kids in a Christian school. Actually, Dan made the decision; I just went along with it because I wanted to learn more about Jesus. In a sense, I was using my kids to spy on Christians!

When I stopped by the school for the initial interview, I ended up lying on the application. I wrote on it that I was a "church-attending Christian," when at the time, I was neither. I thought to myself, *Well, the Whitneys are off to a good start with this whole faith thing. But if I tell the truth, will they even let us through the front door?*

Yep—my pre-Christian motives were just as mixed up as those of the impatient mother-in-law. The only difference: she was a believer; I wasn't.

At the time, being forced to check that box seemed so strange to me. Here was my reasoning: *If Jesus is truly in the hallways of the school, why not let people connect with other people, and then maybe through these kinds of connections, folks will make the decision to go to church on their own?*

It seemed to me that life (and faith) would be a whole lot easier if we didn't have to check those kinds of boxes.

I vividly remember the first time I chose to take someone to coffee instead of attending Bible study. In fact, it stressed me out. I finally got my thinking straight: *I go to Bible study so I can be better at living my faith, not to study the Word and keep it to myself. The women in my study group already know Jesus. This friend doesn't.*

It was better to reach out to my friend—and live my faith.

Lord, I think You would rather we be late for church because we stopped to help a person in need than to see us sitting in the pews, highlighting text. Help me to stop playing church and start being the church. Please fix my crazy motives and get my priorities in line with Yours. Amen.

CHAPTER 7

# LETTING GO OF FEAR

*"Have I not commanded you? Be strong and courageous.*
*Do not be frightened, and do not be dismayed, for*
*the LORD your God is with you wherever you go."*
JOSHUA 1:9 ESV

I used to love hopping in my car and cruising up Interstate 80 toward Omaha, Nebraska. It was a long, peaceful excursion that allowed me to get off the farm for a few hours and away from the demands of motherhood. It was always a treat going into the "big city" to get my hair cut and colored. I'd enjoy the quiet drive past swaying crops and rolling hills with sweet little white churches in the distance. I loved seeing the bright spires pointing high toward heaven.

*This is why I live in the country*, I'd tell myself. *And going into town is fun too!*

But then one day it felt as if my peace was shattered.

I had a health episode about halfway through my trip (I'll spare you the details), and I had to pull on to the shoulder of the road with cars flying by at seventy-five miles an hour. It was scary, and for weeks after that I had the hardest time getting back into the car and making the same road trip. Yet I knew I had to push through. My anxiety was fear-based, and I'm a pretty stubborn person. I don't want anything to get the best of me. I was determined to overcome this, so I kept making hair appointments in Omaha, and I kept asking God for the strength to endure the road trip.

It helped to play worship music and to talk out loud to God as I drove. Yet my anxiety persisted. And then one day my brain began to ping uncontrollably with one stressful thought after another.

PING! *How can I show my kids that I serve a big God if I struggle to get my buns in the car and take a simple road trip on the interstate?*

PING! PING! *Is this a trust issue? By not trusting that God has control over an issue in my life, am I calling Him a liar?*

PING! PING! PING! *I hate it when someone says one thing and then lives another way. Is that what I'm doing? Am I acting like a hypocrite?*

Before I knew it, I was equating my crazy new "I-80 anxiety" with having a shaky witness—and I was becoming fearful about fear, not to mention really, really hard on myself. I suddenly had a lot of stuff to work through.

> I suddenly had a lot of stuff to work through.

Fortunately, 1 John 4:18 came to the rescue: "There is no fear in love. But perfect love drives out fear, because fear has to do with punishment. The one who fears is not made perfect in love."

I had to remind myself that whenever fear rears its ugly head in my life, it's usually because I'm focusing on my situation or my abilities (or lack of them) rather than on God's sovereignty and His attributes. The simple truth is this: in Christ, I don't have to be scared anymore. Now, if I could just get my head to listen to what I know is true in my heart.

.........................................................................................

Lord, I don't want to be scared anymore. I don't want to fear the things of this world or the troubles of the day. And I don't want fear to get in the way of being Your witness. Let Your perfect love drive out fear in my life. Amen.

# CHAPTER 8

# SHARING OUR NEVER-ENDING STORY

*You yourselves are our letter, written on our hearts,*
*known and read by everyone. You show that you are*
*a letter from Christ, the result of our ministry, written*
*not with ink but with the Spirit of the living God, not*
*on tablets of stone but on tablets of human hearts.*

2 CORINTHIANS 3:2–3

I have seven horses on my Nebraska farm, and each one has a unique story.

Not too long ago, just as the sun was starting to drop behind the trees, casting an orange-golden glow on the pastures, I stood on a hill overlooking my farm and thought about a few of those stories. Some in my herd were raised as dressage horses and were trained to compete in equestrian shows. A couple were injured, so their previous owners either couldn't or wouldn't take care of them anymore. One was used as a pack horse. But most of them spent their lives working hard on dusty cattle ranches.

*Of all the horses in the world,* I thought to myself, *these are the ones that retired here with me.* Each animal was so different, so special and funny to me, and I felt blessed to be their caretaker. I took a deep breath and savored my surroundings. A symphony of birds and bugs chirped and squawked and buzzed in the fields. And fanned out everywhere were my beautiful horses—whinnying, grazing, safe and content.

> Fanned out everywhere were my beautiful horses—whinnying, grazing, safe and content.

I couldn't help feeling as if I were living in the pages of one of my favorite childhood books, *Black Beauty.* The novel follows the life of a proud male horse, beginning at birth and ending with his retirement at a "happy place."

As Black Beauty narrates his journey, we learn how his body had been beaten and how he grew weary from the battles of life. And just like us, Beauty had felt abandoned and abused. Yet through it all, he encountered plenty of kind people and loving moments too.

The final chapter is titled "My Last Home"—in which we read about how his strength and spirit were eventually restored.

*This is their happy place,* I told myself as I watched the herd. *It's their final chapter, and I want it to be the best one yet.*

My horses have so many humanlike characteristics—both good and toxic—and I could see a little bit of myself in each one of them. The most heartwarming part of it all was realizing that my horses' stories have become part of my story. Each of us has a unique story to tell: how we got to the places we are, both physically and emotionally, and how God has been with us every step of the way. Truly, life for both beast and man is a wonderful, big adventure.

My husband, who is a committed Christ-follower, grew up attending church. And although he never stopped loving Jesus, he admits he took a few detours. I grew up in a family that did not follow Christ, yet I was

> Truly, life for both beast and man is a wonderful, big adventure.

somehow drawn to Him later in life. As for our kids, they have been set on a positive path toward God, yet I have to admit I often catch myself feeling overwhelmed by the thought of them having to navigate life on their own. What story will they tell by the time they reach their final pasture? How will it end?

I hope they always keep their paths straight. I hope they always follow Christ. So each day I pray, pray, pray for them. But ultimately they belong to a good God who keeps His promises, so I trust Him enough to let them go.

As I grow in my faith, I've come to realize that sharing my story (what some might call my "personal testimony") is hands-down the absolute best way to communicate the gospel with people who don't yet know Jesus.

My story—your story—is truly unique. It's all mine—filled with my very own fingerprints. And it's powerful (even the boring parts). Here's another thought: my story cannot be disputed, because it's my story.

People will always come up with a million excuses about why they don't want anything to do with religion and the church. But they can't argue with my story—or my personal relationship with the God of the universe.

I use my story to share how I went from knowing absolutely nothing about Christ to enthusiastically following Him. I talk about God's miraculous intervention and work in my life through people who shaped me and events that tugged on my heart. I tell why my faith isn't about a religion; it's a growing, changing relationship.

My faith isn't about a religion; it's a growing, changing relationship.

It didn't end the moment I prayed and committed my life to Christ, and it didn't end as I mustered up the courage to step through the doors of a church. In fact, every day I experience new beginnings with Jesus!

Amazing! Our faith story never ends with a conversion experience. It continues all the way up to the day the Lord takes us to greener pastures where, ultimately, our strength and spirit will be restored.

........................................................................................

Lord, thank You for giving me a unique story to share. Help me never be ashamed of it—or You. Let me show that I am a "letter from Christ," the result of Your ministry, "written not with ink but with the Spirit of the living God." Amen.

# CHAPTER 9

# IF THE HAT FITS

*Do your best to present yourself to God as one*
*approved by him, a worker who has no need to be*
*ashamed, rightly explaining the word of truth.*

2 TIMOTHY 2:15 NRSV

I knew I married the right man when he said he liked the smell of cattle haulers. I was putty in his hands! My husband and I like going to live-stock sale barns too. Call us crazy, but we believe a sale-barn cheeseburger is absolute perfection—and I'll fight ya if you think otherwise! Every so often we'll pop into one and make it a lunch date.

Since Dan spent the best parts of his childhood loading hogs into haulers, an afternoon spent at a sale barn always becomes a big social event. He makes his way out to the trucks so he can talk shop with the drivers. That always leaves me holding court and talking cattle with the local high hats.

Dan and I have a running joke: the older a person, the higher their hat. Hence our term of endearment, *high hats*. My grandpa was proof of this. He was in his eighties when he passed away, and during his last days on earth, his hat was sitting on the very top of his head. I'm baffled how he kept it there. It made me wonder if old-age wisdom swells our noggins!

My husband can't believe how I'm able to keep up with these old sale-barn guys. I tell him, "I don't need to be wearing a high hat to talk about cattle." I'm passionate about what I do know, so I think these guys get a kick out of all five foot three inches of me and my farming adventures.

I recently had a really encouraging talk with a friend who had been praying for her older brothers since she was in the seventh grade. My friend is now in her forties, so that's a mighty long time to be praying for lost souls. But she never quit! A few weeks back, one of her brothers started going to church. He has even been passing biblical nuggets on to his older brother, who has been battling health issues. What a great reminder that God is always working to bring us home, and He's orchestrating something amazing in the lives of this family. My friend's steady faith and consistent lifestyle have been the greatest witnesses of all. Now her brother is eager to make a change.

It's a good reminder that you don't have to know everything about the Bible to speak the gospel, because the gospel message is simple enough for a child to understand. Don't get me wrong; training to evangelize is extremely helpful. (I mean, here I am offering a book about it.) But we don't need to wait until we are experts before we have the right to tell others that Jesus loves them. Young or old, novice or theologian, the evangelism hat is one-size-fits-all. We just need a caring, willing heart to share Christ with others. My friend's brother isn't even technically a believer yet and he's already planting some seeds.

Jesus wants each of us to have a childlike faith—the kind that is pure, unassuming, and humble. I think Teddy Roosevelt summed up a lot of things when he said, "Comparison is the thief of joy."[1] Too often we compare ourselves to others—everything from our IQ and appearance to our spiritual lives. And as we do this, we end up feeling inadequate.

We look around church and start thinking that maybe the person sitting across the aisle is better equipped to share their faith. We assume they know a whole lot more than us. But think about this: the Bible is filled with plenty of everyday, ordinary people who God entrusted to share the gospel.

Most of the disciples did not come from much. These were men who were more comfortable on a fishing boat than standing before the scholarly Jewish Sanhedrin, a sort of high council. They had every reason to feel intimidated by their accusers. But, amazingly, the Sanhedrin was dumbfounded by the boldness and spiritual wisdom of these uneducated men. (See the verses about Peter and John before the Sanhedrin in Acts 4–6.)

What made the difference? The disciples were convinced of the one thing that matters most in life: Jesus died and rose again so that we can be saved.

The gospel is as simple and as profound as that.

If we're passionate about what we know, then the hat fits. We can wear it proudly.

........................................................................................

Lord, fill me with the boldness to share the gospel and the spiritual wisdom to rightly explain the word of truth. I want to be "one approved" by You. Amen.

# CHAPTER 10

# IT'S *NOT* ABOUT HOW GOOD WE ARE

*A man came up to him, saying, "Teacher, what good deed*
*must I do to have eternal life?" And he said to him, "Why do*
*you ask me about what is good? There is only one who is good.*
*If you would enter life, keep the commandments." He said to*
*him, "Which ones?" And Jesus said, "You shall not murder,*
*You shall not commit adultery, You shall not steal, You shall*
*not bear false witness, Honor your father and mother, and,*
*You shall love your neighbor as yourself." The young man*
*said to him, "All these I have kept. What do I still lack?"*
MATTHEW 19:16–20 ESV

Everyone who loves horses remembers that one special four-legged friend that completely changed their life. I, too, owned such a horse. My Roanie was so good to me; she watched out for me on the trail, and she even carried me unscathed on her back when we accidentally stumbled on a hive of bees.

In my book, Roanie hung the moon. That's how I'll always remember her. Yet I must admit, she had her fair share of saltiness. Roanie often didn't get along with other horses, so she had to be trailered separately.

I must admit something else: I was a lot like Roanie. Before I became a Christian, I sometimes didn't get along with people and preferred the company of horses. And I had my fair share of salty days too!

Shortly after becoming a Christian, I couldn't stop talking about my faith. I was full of joy and excitement about knowing Jesus. It was like owing a debt that I knew I could never pay back and then finding out that debt had been paid in full. And it was definitely like being on death row my whole life and then suddenly learning I had received a full pardon.

I was bursting at the seams . . . only to have icy cold water thrown in my face by a skeptical friend. A guy I'd known for many years just didn't understand the change I'd made. In fact, he looked at me differently from that point on. He saw no reason for a "savior" in his life because he considered himself to be a good person. And that's how he saw me too. "You're already good," he said, "so what are you being saved from? And how can a 'savior' possibly help you?"

"But I am *not* good," I kept telling him. "I'm a sinner, and so are you—along with every man, woman, and child who ever lived. We all fall short because of sin that's come into the world. That's why we need *the* Savior."

He didn't understand, and because I was a brand-new believer, I had a hard time articulating my thoughts. That conversation's always bothered me. I felt like I missed an opportunity to give my friend a clear delivery of the gospel. Sadly, we grew apart, partly because I became a Christian and partly because he married an atheist.

A few years later, a mutual friend of ours passed away. That opened another opportunity to witness to him, but now with confidence. I got in touch with him after the funeral, and we had a really good conversation about the sadness of death and the joy of eternal life. He still wasn't interested (he said he's now an atheist too), but at least he has heard the whole truth. I am so thankful for another chance, and even though it came with sad circumstances, he was able to see how precious and fragile human life is. In his weakness, I delivered the gospel. Now the rest is between him and God.

If you ask most people what we have to do to get to heaven, the overwhelming response will be some form of what my friend once believed: "We need to be good people."

We should live in such a way that others will want to know what makes us different. In fact, I have met Christians who use their lives as the sole means of evangelizing, but I think we need to be careful about that. We can certainly reveal the character of Christ through patience, love, kindness, and self-control, but without introducing Christ Himself—and what He did for each one of us—I wonder if an unbeliever may just conclude we're really nice people.

Salvation is by faith alone, through grace alone, in Christ alone. That is such awesome news for everyone who understands and accepts it. But we have to make sure the people we speak to about Jesus understand why the gospel is so mind-blowing. To do that, we must start with the bad news.

The Old Testament law was given to Israel during the time of Moses. This law is the measuring stick, and sin is anything that falls short of perfection according to that standard.

Jesus addressed the rich young ruler's question, "What do I still lack?" by pointing out that only people as good as God could earn a right standing with Him. In other words, only those who have kept the law perfectly. Yet there ain't nobody as good as God!

So it doesn't matter how good we try to be. The Bible says, "For all have sinned and fall short of the glory of God" (Romans 3:23). The next verse tells us, "All are justified freely by his grace through the redemption that came by Christ Jesus" (v. 24). In other words, the *only* way to spend eternity with God in heaven is to accept the forgiveness Jesus offers us. That's why Christ going to the cross on our behalf is the greatest news ever.

We don't have to worry about whether we've been good enough to get into heaven, because it's *not* about how good we are. It's all about knowing, loving, and following Jesus.

That's the good news we need to communicate.

Lord, You are God—my Lord and Savior. I praise You, I love You, and I thank You for paying the price for my sin and giving me eternal life. Help me communicate this good news everywhere I go and with everyone I meet. Amen.

# CHAPTER 11

# NO DOUBT ABOUT IT . . . GOD CAN BE TRUSTED

*You are the one and only LORD. You made the heavens. You
made even the highest heavens. You created all the stars
in the sky. You created the earth and everything on it. And
you made the oceans and everything in them. You give life
to everything. Every living being in heaven worships you.*
NEHEMIAH 9:6 NIRV

My larger-than-average Norwegian Fjord horse, Gus, is a beast of a boy. He's shaggy, and his forelock completely covers his eyes. He reminds me a lot of Sam Sheepdog from the old Looney Tunes cartoons. Gus is even missing a few teeth. But don't let this rough exterior and his odd-smelling body keep you from seeing what's in his heart. Once you earn his trust, Gus is one of the sweetest horses you'll ever meet.

Gus and I have been through a lot together.

When I first met him, he was used for packing elk meat out of the woods during hunting trips, and he carried gear as well. It must have been his large size that made him the ideal candidate for the job of pack mule, but I saw something more in Gus. I decided that maybe he would prefer to pull things rather than carry them. It was Gus's demeanor that inspired the idea, even though others were skeptical. So I purchased a cart and enrolled us both in carriage-driving lessons—something that neither one of us had ever done before. It was challenging, to say the least, and we both fought back at different times (but luckily not at the same time, or I may have given up).

It's like I tell my husband about marriage, "Only one of us is allowed to be crazy at a time." And just like marriage, Gus and I became closer as we weathered hard times as a team.

> It's like I tell my husband about marriage, "Only one of us is allowed to be crazy at a time."

Gus and I both had our doubts, but we pressed on—and were ready to compete in our first carriage-driving show about a year later. We didn't take the whole enchilada in competition, but we did place with ribbons, and we left with our heads held high. Gus the Fjord isn't just a pack horse. Gus is capable of so much more!

God knows us better than we know ourselves, so He truly sees that we, too, are capable of so much more. When we are in the will of God, He is going to prompt us into action on His behalf. It's not always in ways we might expect, but it will always be in ways that push us to evangelize and bring glory to Him.

He usually seems to ask us to do things that stretch the parts of ourselves that we struggle with. He has called me to write even though I've struggled my entire life with feelings of being academically inadequate. Recently God called a friend of mine to lead a ministry even though she feels that organization and planning aren't in her wheelhouse. Then again, maybe they are. God sees something there. I wonder if my friend was criticized early in life for being disorganized, so now she believes what others told her.

God wants us to trust Him, not the labels people slap on us.

The Enemy would love for us to get stuck in negative thinking and wrong beliefs about ourselves. And why wouldn't he? That keeps us trapped in fear and paralyzed when we have opportunities to share our faith in Christ. The Enemy even makes us doubt our own salvation. He dumps so much insecurity on us that we can't help feeling as if we're helplessly floundering in a grave, with a steady load of doubt being shoveled onto our heads.

God wants us to trust Him, not the labels people slap on us.

One thing's for sure: the gospel message is 100 percent trustworthy and true. If it weren't, the Enemy wouldn't fight so hard to keep us quiet about it. The Devil's tactic is pretty clever, when you think about it. Toxic people follow the same tactic. They create doubt and confusion, causing us to question ourselves. Suddenly we tell ourselves that we'll get to the task of evangelizing later. Or we may tell ourselves something like, *I am so full of shame that I have no business telling others about Jesus.*

But who better than you?

We have a trustworthy Father who sees more in us than we see in ourselves. If we keep our minds on Scripture and our hearts soft, we'll never lose concern for the souls of other people whom God loves. He will supply all we need for the task He calls on us to do.

God partners with us because it helps us grow spiritually, and it makes us become closer and more dependent on Him.

I have to be super transparent with you: I, too, wake up many days shrouded with doubt and the belief that I am not capable of much. But I also choose to ignore that voice and continue to move forward regardless. My armpits sweat and my stomach knots up, but my belief that God tells the truth helps me take that first step, and then a second one, and a third.

I remind myself that David won the battle against Goliath because he had faith and believed that God tells the truth. If that battle didn't include David's dependence on God, I know a boy could never slay a giant on his own.

My beautiful Norwegian Fjord horse is capable of so much more. And so are you and I!

..................................................................................

Lord, thank You for being a good, good Father. Thank You for seeing that there is more in me than I could ever think possible. You created each one of us to bring glory to You. If You believe I'm up for the task, help me believe it too. Amen.

# CHAPTER 12

# DOZING DISCIPLES

*He returned to his disciples and found them*
*sleeping. "Couldn't you men keep watch with*
*me for one hour?" he asked Peter.*

MATTHEW 26:40

What does a country girl look like? My husband, Dan, says that I'm the real deal. I guess I'd have to agree with him, having grown up on a cattle farm and riding horses my whole life. What Dan gets a kick out of is that I don't look the part. I live in Converse Chucks, T-shirts, and jeans. I appear to be more skater than cowgirl.

I once hired a guy to train my horse. Now, this guy really captured the part—total cowboy from his wide-brimmed Stetson all the way down to the spurs on his boots. But six months later, my horse was no better trained than when he started. He apparently looked the part but lacked the action.

It's like that for Christ-followers too—especially when it comes to prayer.

I encounter lots of people on social media who comfort others by saying things like, "You're in my prayers." Do you think they're actually praying, or are they just trying to make themselves feel better or sound more spiritual? I ask this because I'm guilty of it too.

Then I realized that saying we're praying but not actually doing it is just as ineffective as saying, "I'm sending you positive vibes." These are do-nothing words that lack action.

How important is prayer? Christ yearned for support in prayer during His darkest hour. But do you remember what the disciples did? Here Jesus was going to take on the sin of the world, and they fell asleep.

When someone is in pain, we have a choice to either act like those disciples and sleep on it or come alongside our friends, get on our knees, and pray for their burden. Whether they are in Christ or not, hurting people appreciate prayer. The action of praying shows others true concern for their circumstances, and it's a great way to share Christ.

> When someone is in pain, we have a choice to either act like those disciples and sleep on it or come alongside our friends, get on our knees, and pray for their burden.

I have been in situations in which people have been so broken, they've asked me to pray for them. You know what I do? I set the alarm on my phone—say for 8:00 a.m. or 5:30 p.m., whenever they need prayer the most—and then I have them do the same on their phone. This way they'll know the exact time I'm lifting them up in prayer. This simple, selfless act usually means so much to someone in need.

Apathy suffocates the body of Christ, and it slows down the work of truth. All it takes for the Enemy to gain a foothold is for us to do nothing. If a building is on fire, I don't just stand there and watch it burn. When someone is hurting from the sudden loss of a loved one, I need to jump into action. The danger is real for those who don't know Christ yet. I can pray over their circumstance and introduce them to the Savior all at the same time.

So whenever I read about the disciples falling asleep instead of praying, I remind myself of all the times when I've done that. I think about all the missed opportunities, and then I make an effort to be a prayer warrior instead of a dozing disciple.

What does a good disciple look like? You and me, in action.

Lord, I don't want to just look the part of a Christ-follower and wrap my faith in a bunch of nice-sounding words and good intentions. I want to be the real deal. Help me be a person of action—loving, praying, serving, and sharing. Amen.

# CHAPTER 13

# CALVES IN JACKETS

*Surely I know the plans I have for you, says
the Lord, plans for your welfare and not for
harm, to give you a future with hope.*
JEREMIAH 29:11 NRSV

Recently I saw an article claiming that farmers don't have much compassion for their animals. I can tell you from firsthand experience, that accusation could not be further from the truth. Most farmers do all they can to ensure their livestock are well taken care of. Between staying up all night tending to a calving heifer to making sure every creature is fed and water isn't frozen as temperatures hit the negatives, most farmers treat their animals like family.

Back in Wisconsin, when I was a kid, the very first weeks of calving season were met with at least one inevitable blizzard. Since we had more cows than room in our barn, that created a problem. But to my clever mom, every problem presents a solution. She just happened to be a talented seamstress, so one of her many remedies for keeping newborns warm was to create several bovine-friendly jackets. Can you picture it? Calves in jackets! And it worked.

One of her many remedies for keeping newborns warm was to create several bovine-friendly jackets.

Before concocting her brilliant jacket solution, we had to warm up each little guy in our family's bathtub. I remember my baby sister writing a story for school about a calf that lived in our bathtub. Her teacher must have thought she had an amazingly creative mind, which she did. Yet it was just another typical day in the life of a farm kid. (I chuckle every time I imagine the calf in the tub, watching my sister brush her teeth before school!)

Mom's calf jackets were made from a rainproof fabric with a fuzzy liner sewn inside. They went over the back of the calf and wrapped around its chest with straps. Their little heads stuck out through a hole in the front. Each one did the trick, ensuring the calf's body heat didn't escape up top. They would wear these until we had some consistent days of dry weather. Then we would catch the calf and take the coat off, and the sun would do the warming for us. It was always so funny to see those little guys out in the field wearing their calf jackets, happily bucking up and down and chasing after their mothers.

These are good memories of farm life, for sure, so when I hear people say farmers don't care about their animals, I bristle a bit. We loved ours so much, my mom made clothes for them!

God also gets accused of not caring about us.

That, too, could not be further from the truth. I know that when good people slam into tough times (and don't understand why), sometimes it's really easy to blame God. It's also hard to understand (and accept) when bad people receive good things. It's almost as if God is rewarding them for bad behavior.

Last winter I was mindlessly clicking through the TV channels when I landed on a documentary about serial killer Jeffrey Dahmer. I tuned in halfway through the show, so I cannot tell you everything that it was about, but by the time Dan had made it back inside the house after smoking a cigar outside, I was weeping openly.

> It's . . . hard to understand (and accept) when bad people receive good things.

Jeffrey had given his life to the Lord just before he died. I was genuinely happy for him, and his family was overtaken with joy by the truth that no one is beyond the reach of God.

Minister Roy Ratcliff, who conducted Jeffrey Dahmer's funeral service on December 2, 1994, eulogized Dahmer and said,

> Jeff confessed to me his great remorse for his crimes. He wished he could do something for the families of his victims to make it right, but there was nothing he could do. He turned to God because there was no one else to turn to, but he showed great courage in his daring to ask the question, "Is heaven for me too?" I think many people are resentful of him for asking that question. But he dared to ask, and he dared to believe the answer.[1]

We should have the heart to want to see everyone saved, including a serial killer. I personally want everyone to experience the joy of knowing that they are not on this earth by mistake; they are loved by their Creator, and it is never too late for them to experience that relationship while they are drawing breath. Seeing people saved overtakes me.

But also I was moved by something Jeffrey's stepmother said on the documentary:

Seeing people saved overtakes me.

> You love the sinner, not the sin. . . . If you look at the first trial pictures, you see Jeff in lousy clothes. Well, Lionel and I got up there and literally took the suit off of Lionel's back, shoes, shirt and tie and we gave them to Jeff. So that he can go to court looking decent. [But] he knew there was no way we [could] condone what he did.[2]

That hit me in the feels!

If there was ever an absolute picture of what God's grace looks like, it was in that statement from the stepmother of a serial killer who had never stopped loving her son despite his actions. I think there are probably people who have a hard time with God's amazing grace for someone like Jeffrey Dahmer. To someone who doesn't understand the Lord's grace, it appears as though he was being rewarded for bad behavior.

To be good witnesses for Christ, we must know that God's grace is almost beyond our comprehension. It's the unmerited favor of God— much, much more than a prayer before a meal. His grace is this: God sending His only Son to die as a criminal so that God's enemies might live. God's grace looks like the stepmother of a serial killer making sure her child is made decent in a suit despite his actions.

God loves His children so much He fashioned a way for you and me to be made decent. It's unfair and unmerited, and it's a message that continues to change the world. It inspires us to have a heart for lost people and encourages us to tell others that God's grace is a gift for everyone who has the courage to ask, "Is heaven for me too?"

..........................................................................................

Lord, thank You that not one of us is too bad or too late to be forgiven. Thank You for caring about every detail of our lives—especially for Your plans for our welfare and not for harm—so we can have an eternal future filled with hope. Amen.

# CHAPTER 14

# GOD CAN FIX A CRAZY LIFE

*Don't be deceived, my dear brothers and sisters. Every good*
*and perfect gift is from above, coming down from the Father*
*of the heavenly lights, who does not change like shifting*
*shadows. He chose to give us birth through the word of truth,*
*that we might be a kind of firstfruits of all he created.*
JAMES 1:16–18

There's this guy in the city who sings everywhere—coffeehouses, street corners, music festivals, churches . . . anywhere he can draw a crowd. His voice has that gritty edge, and his songs churn up all kinds of emotions in those who listen. They make you think. Even cry.

His beat-up, twelve-string guitar looks like a yard-sale reject: it's covered with surfing stickers, duct tape, and "graffiti" from friends (notes, doodles, and autographs). Amazingly, though, he manages to pull incredible beauty out of something so ugly.

This guy is talented, yet—like his guitar—his life is pretty messy.

It started out that way.

This guy is talented, yet—like his guitar—his life is pretty messy.

His mom and dad abandoned him when he was a small boy, pawning him off on his grandparents. There he was, just out of diapers and barely able to talk, and his young heart was already torn and bruised. He actually started believing that he was so unlovable, so flawed, that his parents couldn't stand to be around him. And when they ended up getting a divorce, he blamed himself for that too. Slowly a toxic mix of shame, self-loathing, and rage began to bubble inside.

Things got messier through the years, mostly because of alcohol and drug abuse during his teen years. He plunged deep into the Rastafari movement as a young man, searching for meaning to his life, but he ended up becoming more confused (not to mention really, really high all the time). He hit rock bottom at age twenty-four and spent time behind bars for using and dealing drugs.

And then he met Jesus.

After that, everything began to fall in place . . . right? He did a "Christian 180," and now he has a perfect life.

Not exactly.

Despite ten years of "trying to get things right," his life is still pretty messy.

He reads his Bible, he prays, he devours every spiritual growth book he can get his hands on, he serves in church, he hangs out with Christ-following friends—he does all kinds of Christian things that Christians are supposed to do, and yet he still slips on life's messes and falls flat on his face.

In fact, he's even dealing with some new twists to a bunch of old problems: abandonment (this time by his wife), divorce (this time his own), and imprisonment (this time by his emotions). As for that toxic shame thing, it's still pooling and swirling inside. On some occasions, usually during weak moments, it gets the best of him. Old habits and negative ways of thinking seem to take over, and before he realizes it, he has lost the day spiritually.

> He does all kinds of Christian things that Christians are supposed to do, and yet he still slips on life's messes and falls flat on his face.

Here's what's changed during his decade of walking with Jesus: he doesn't try to hide his mess. He's actually pretty open about it, and he even writes songs about the things that trip him up. This brings out a sigh of relief in some believers who have heard his story. *I'm not alone!* they tell themselves. *I can stop pretending that I have it all together, and I can start living with authenticity just like this guy. I don't have to be afraid anymore. I can take a step toward God, warts and all.*

Others, though, write off his life as yet another depressing story and even label him hypocritical, phony, or backslidden.

I think we should lean toward the first group, knowing that God can fix a crazy life. That's the hope in Christ we need to communicate.

Following Christ is about authenticity, not performance. It's more about the everyday journey than a level of achievement. Even though your hang-ups and my hang-ups may be different from this guy's, the fact is, we all still get hung up from time to time. Even as Christ-followers, we don't always keep it together. And if we're honest with ourselves, we know:

*We have a messy faith and a messy life.*
*We fall flat on our faces—more often than we care to admit.*
*We desperately need a Savior.*

Following Christ is about authenticity, not performance.

If we're honest with ourselves, we know we're all a little bit like this guy.

"There are a lot of broken people in this world," he once said. "I'd say that *all* are broken, but only a few admit it. We like to believe we're okay—that we have it all together; it makes us feel better about ourselves. I've learned that it's okay to be broken. When we get to this point, we can put away all the junk that gets in the way—our efforts to 'get things right,' and to 'do Christian things' . . . our pride, our stubborn wills, our attempts to control everything and everyone. God is our Healer. He can accomplish in us what we cannot do on our own."[1]

Wise words we need to share with a broken and hurting world.

. . . . . . . . . . . . . . . . . . . . . . . . . . . . . . . . . . . . . . . . . . . . . . . . . . . . . . . . . . . . . . . . . . . . . . . . . . . . . . . . .

Lord, I know we're all broken, and we all need You. Thank You for fixing my sometimes-crazy life. Don't let me get buried in shame; rather, let it help me communicate Your hope with a broken world. Bring people on my path who need a healing touch. Empower me to love, share, and care. Amen.

# CHAPTER 15

# JESUS CAN BE PUZZLING

*"God so loved the world, that He gave His only*
*Son, so that everyone who believes in Him*
*will not perish, but have eternal life."*
JOHN 3:16 NASB

T he farm goes into hibernation during winter. The crops are in, the round bales are out, and the horses are wrapped in their thick winter coats. Everything slows down.

For me, snowfall is not only welcome, it's exciting to anticipate. I can't wait to look out the window on a blustery Nebraska day and watch fluffy, jewellike ice crystals swirl and dance and dart around before they settle on the ground. Like shimmering pieces of a puzzle, those tiny snowflakes meld together and transform our farm into a Currier and Ives postcard! They decorate groves of pine and elm trees that mark our property line; they ice over a gazebo by the creek—the very spot where Dan and I were married; they blanket rolling fields where beanstalks once sprang up weeks before the harvest.

Inside our house, life slows down too. Everyone is warm and cozy with a roaring fire blazing on the hearth. My kids are usually planted in front of the TV, wrapped up like mummies in blankets and munching on popcorn or something sweeter. I usually opt for something sweeter too. Since, at this point in the year, it's way too early to think about weight gain, I often allow myself to enjoy a cup or two (or three) of hot cocoa. And why not? Swimsuit season is months away!

As the first snowfall changes life on our farm, I begin one of my favorite holiday traditions, something I've been doing since my childhood in Wisconsin. I clear off the dining room table and pull out a thousand-piece mystery puzzle, one with a picture on the box that doesn't match its final image.

Since . . . it's way too early to think about weight gain, I often allow myself to enjoy a cup or two (or three) of hot cocoa.

At the beginning, I don't know what the puzzle will look like, but by the time Christmas arrives, my masterpiece will emerge. It'll be a cute picture with a title like "Springtime on the Farm" or "Kittens in a Basket." If I'm lucky, I'll piece together "A Currier and Ives Christmas."

The tradition is always the same, and it's always exciting to anticipate!

Years ago, when my kids were toddlers, I was cocky enough with my parenting abilities to think I could build a puzzle while they sat with me at the table. Never try this. Puzzle pieces were scattered everywhere. It was chaos! My children grabbed at my sorted piles of colors like a drowning man grabs at a life preserver.

Thankfully, it's a much more tranquil scene today. Now I can sit for hours, calmly sorting through oddly shaped puzzle pieces, with one eye on my hobby and the other on the snowflakes out my window. And at moments like these, my mind inevitably wanders to another passion of mine—one that's just as puzzling: sharing Jesus in a world that's confused about faith.

How can someone believe in God if they can't grasp the big picture? It's sort of like not seeing the image on the box before you commit to taking on a thousand-piece puzzle.

How can someone
believe in God if they can't
grasp the big picture?

People who have little or no background with spiritual matters often feel just as overwhelmed. So I don't find it hard to relate to them at all. It wasn't until I was in my twenties when I connected Easter with the Christian faith. I thought it was all about brightly colored eggs and fuzzy bunnies. And I am pretty sure (without having to bother a statistician) that a lack of knowledge of anything spiritual is becoming more and more common these days. To the unchurched, there is a belief that all religions lead to the same God and that all faiths teach the same things. So if I'm a nice person, I will make it to *my* version of heaven.

This is what I believed—at least the part of me that hoped that God was real. The other part of me just wasn't sure.

The Bible supports the idea that every person inherently understands that there is a God. We are surrounded by His handiwork, and His invisible attributes can clearly be seen if we choose to look. Solomon said that humanity was created for eternity, which leads to our longing for something beyond this world (Ecclesiastes 3:11). Since we bear God's image, we can't help but yearn to reconnect with Him. I can tell you from experience, this is true. Still, I'd often suppress those feelings. Thankfully God has His ways of getting our attention and making Himself known.

As we reach out to unbelieving friends and loved ones, we can tap into this innate longing. Yet we need to remember that not everyone has been exposed to the basics. And here's something else to think about: Christianity can be puzzling!

I'll never forget the first time I heard the phrase about being "covered in the blood." *Blood?* I wondered. *What's the blood? And whose blood is it?*

It sounded weird and gross, and it made me think of that Stephen King story in which a girl named Carrie was covered in pig's blood. I hadn't heard the Bible stories, and I didn't know who Jesus claimed to be. I literally thought He was God's kid or something—not God in human form. I was clueless.

So what's a better approach as we share? Introduce folks to the Creator Himself before we scare them away with Christianese. Come to think of it, maybe we should just stop using Christianese altogether.

> I hadn't heard the Bible stories, and I didn't know who Jesus claimed to be.

A friend of mine recently tried witnessing to her nephew over the summer and was disappointed that as this young man took one step toward Christ, he'd retreat and would even back up two steps. Here's what I told my friend: "If your nephew has never even been given the opportunity to ponder whether or not God exists, he can't be expected to see a need for a Savior—especially since, at his age, he probably feels as though he hasn't done anything bad enough to warrant salvation."

I can almost guarantee that the young man's perception of God is that of an old, gray-bearded grandfather—the rules guy who is constantly telling the riffraff to stay off his lawn. So helping my friend's nephew put the puzzle together starts by "putting the gospel on him." In other words, she needs to make the introduction to who God is: "In the beginning God created the heavens and the earth" (Genesis 1:1).

Once her nephew begins to believe this, everything else is possible.

Now my friend can introduce him to the true character of God: He is good, and He can be trusted.

I love watching my mystery masterpiece slowly emerge right before my eyes. And I love what happens each winter right outside my window: tiny shimmering crystals meld together, transforming a hibernating farm into a snowy wonderland!

> I love what happens each winter right outside my window: tiny shimmering crystals meld together.

My persistence with puzzles relates to how I share my faith.

As I build the outside of the puzzle first, then I have a place where all of the other pieces can begin fitting in place. So with my faith, I can build off the idea that a good God had a plan from the beginning, and it was a beautiful plan until the selfish toddlers entered the room and the whole thing went awry.

And by the way, *we* are those selfish toddlers.

My friend should be encouraged by the fact that her nephew—right along with the rest of the unchurched world—probably doesn't have an overly hardened heart toward God. So patience is key. Some puzzles take a little longer to put together than others. It may take years, months, or, in my case, decades. The key is consistency, because the world is constantly bombarding them with all kinds of lies. Our job is to always make sure we put the pieces together in a room with strong and truthful lighting. Growing up without a knowledge of theology means they've never encountered any bad theology. They've never had the unfortunate experience of growing up in a denomination that causes more long-term harm than good. Bad-lighting situations sometimes make us end up with pieces of the puzzle that don't truly fit because they were pushed down too hard. When this happens, we end up tearing the puzzle piece as we pull it out to restart the build.

But the good news says that once people get introduced to Jesus' part in the story, they will realize that the price was paid in full by the perfect mediator. The foundation is laid for reconciliation. Salvation doesn't just involve the forgiveness of sin. It also brings sinners into relationship with God.

Jesus is that lost piece of the puzzle—the piece you can so satisfyingly push into that empty space in your heart, the missing piece where it all comes together to make a big, beautiful picture. One that's even better than the picture on the box.

Lord Jesus, help me remember how faith looks and feels to people who have no knowledge of You. Show me how to love them the way You love them. Amen.

# CHAPTER 16

# LET'S KEEP IT REAL

*By grace you have been saved through faith. And this is not
your own doing; it is the gift of God, not a result of works,
so that no one may boast. For we are his workmanship,
created in Christ Jesus for good works, which God
prepared beforehand, that we should walk in them.*

EPHESIANS 2:8–10 ESV

I was digging through a box of old photos the other day, looking for a picture of my dad. I have dozens of shots of him, so this shouldn't have taken up my entire afternoon, yet it did. That's because stuffed inside the box were endless photos of my kids as itty-bitty people, and snapshot after snapshot of my husband and me as brand-new parents.

I couldn't resist looking at each one of them!

Time was frozen on each glossy piece of paper. And I couldn't believe what I was seeing. No gray hairs or worry lines. Maybe some tired eyes—but that just comes with the territory, right? What I loved most were the candid shots of our kids just being kids—running, jumping, enjoying crazy adventures that were caught on film. I loved their dirty faces, ear-to-ear smiles, and bug bites covering their tiny arms and legs!

I pulled out a shot of our daughter with a goose egg on her head, and I groaned out loud. *Ouch! I remember that one.*

My mind instantly flashed back to what I'd told my husband as we were bringing our firstborn home from the hospital: "This is insane! They'll let anyone have kids."

> "This is insane! They'll let anyone have kids."

All the fears and worries about becoming a parent came rushing back to me, which made me chuckle. *Why on earth was I so worried?* I mean, honestly—now that my kids are on the brink of becoming teenagers, the toddler years seem like a cake walk!

Each photo was a good reminder that God's got us covered.

As I sat on the floor in our den sorting through my box of memories, I was struck by another realization: I adored all the raw and real memories and seemed to flip right past the picture-perfect shots that I wasted so much time trying to orchestrate. The more authentic the moment, the more I connected with the photo. I think it's that way in life too.

God continues to take my messy moments and helps me grow and even blossom. Best of all, He uses my imperfect, real-life moments to steer other imperfect people toward a relationship with Him. Through Jesus, we can live life more abundantly but also with more authenticity.

We hear people say, "Let's keep it real." Yet how often do we actually live this way?

In this day and age of social media, it's hard to let things go out into the world without filtering them first. We like to share the flawless, edited versions of ourselves; the ideal—how we would like things to be. I am guilty of this too—especially of not letting photos of my aging face, lumpy middle-aged body, and less-than-perfect kids go out for all to see.

Yet just as I flipped right past the picture-perfect shots in my memory box, I bond with people who aren't afraid to show their blemishes. That happened just the other day at Sam's Club. As I perused the entertainment aisle, another mom shared

> We like to share the flawless, edited versions of ourselves.

that her son spends too much time playing video games. (So does mine!) Her authenticity made us instant friends. It encouraged me and helped me realize that I wasn't alone. And the two of us, perfect strangers, started conversing about different ways we could encourage our boys, and each other, to make a change.

Regardless of how often we pose for a photo—turning our good side toward the camera—and regardless of how much we "edit" ourselves on Facebook, we're all imperfect.

There are days we don't feel spiritual, and moments when we act like jerks. There are days I tell myself, *So and so needs to hear this sermon*, and then I realize that I'm being a self-righteous clown. *Ugh!*

Here's the beauty of the gospel: God uses imperfect people to reach other imperfect people. Together, we grow. Sharing our blemishes can help someone who isn't yet a Christian realize that following Jesus isn't about being perfect or even good. Jesus offers Himself to us because we can never be good enough. God's grace is abundant. And I think it's really encouraging to know that God can still use us in spite of the fact we're all such abysmal works in progress.

So here's what keeping it real means to me: I admit that sometimes I lose it over the phone with someone from the cable company. Sometimes I get scared and begin to worry when I know I shouldn't. Sometimes I don't feel as if I measure up. The truth is, if a measuring stick of Christ's life were laid alongside ours, it would reveal a lot of failure on our part. Our lack of worship, our bad attitudes, our level of commitment.

> It's really encouraging to know that God can still use us in spite of the fact we're all such abysmal works in progress.

Looking through that box of photos made me realize I can't orchestrate a perfect-looking life, and to try and do so makes me more like a "poser." I'd rather be real. Those imperfect photos represent more than what I could have ever expected or anticipated in this life: redemption that I do not deserve.

Jesus tells us that the abundant life is a continual process of learning, practicing, and maturing. We will fail, recover, adjust, and overcome. I am going to try to be more purposeful about taking the filters off my life so I can show others why I need Jesus—and why they need Him too.

.......................................................................................

Lord, I know we're all imperfect. Help me be real with You and those I encounter every day. Let others see Your perfect love through my imperfect life. Amen.

# CHAPTER 17

# COURTNEY'S CASSEROLE

*"If you love me, obey my commands. I will ask the Father.*
*And he will give you another friend to help you and to be*
*with you forever. That friend is the Spirit of truth. The*
*world can't accept him. That's because the world does*
*not see him or know him. But you know him. He lives*
*with you, and he will be in you. I will not leave you like*
*children who don't have parents. I will come to you."*
JOHN 14:15–18 NIRV

When I was a kid, long before cell phones took over the world, the big craze was CB radios. Remember them?

I could sit for hours reliving a *Convoy* moment. *"Break-19 . . . you got your ears on?"* I'd imagine myself telling my big-rig buddies. *"You've got a plain brown wrapper on your back door. And just eyeballed bear in the bushes. Back it down and keep the shiny side up. Movin' on . . . 10-4."*

Along with the fun lingo, I loved the crazy handles (names) people would give themselves: Rubber Duck, Pack Rat, Silver Streak,

Eighteen-Wheel Eddie, Sod Buster, Road Hog, Broken Bunny, High Plains Drifter, Sassy Kat.

While CBs have mostly gone the way of disco balls and bell-bottom jeans, plenty of diehard truckers out there will never pull a "10–3" with their radios. (That's trucker-talk for "they'll never stop transmitting.") Hollywood has immortalized the CB world, but there's a practical side to it. During the seventies and early eighties—without cell phones and GPS—it was the only way the heavy haulers could communicate with each other. Even today, as they rumble down the backroads and byways of this vast, beautiful land, technology isn't always reliable. Sometimes the old-school ways work best. Sometimes truckers go back to the basics so they can keep their ears on.

Believe it or not, it's like that as we tune in to the Holy Spirit.

Keeping my ears on is a good way to glean what I call "biblical nuggets" from life. And it's a great way for the Holy Spirit to speak to me exactly what I need to hear at a specific moment in time. These things deepen my faith, and they refine me.

> Keeping my ears on is a good way to glean what I call "biblical nuggets" from life.

As I was mindlessly perusing social media one afternoon, one of my buddies, Courtney, posted something that hit me so profoundly it stopped me in my tracks. But instead of receiving a biblical nugget, I felt as if I was treated to a whole meal—what I call "Courtney's Casserole." Her words were filled with such meatiness, they gave me wisdom that I can apply to life's hard moments. And without realizing it, Courtney showed me how to show up and be Christ to someone who is facing a really bad day.

After losing her dad unexpectedly, she wrote about how the Christmas season just wasn't the same anymore. She mourned the memories of her father—the laughter, the fun, the warm moments the two once shared. But then one holiday season when she felt particularly depressed, she received a Holy Spirit nudge in the form of some frank, "get-your-ears-on" motherly advice. Here's what Courtney's mom had told her: "I can get through the holidays when I remind myself that Christmas really isn't about me or

our traditions or the things that make us feel comfortable and loved. . . . You have to adjust your perspective. It's all about *Him*. Period."

That's a big 10–4! I felt that nudge too, and I heard the Holy Spirit loud and clear.

Touching another life with Christ's love isn't about me. It isn't about saying the right words at the right time. It's about *Him*. Period.

At times in life, we can't help feeling as if we're on a weary, long haul and that we just don't have anything left in us to give. Yet it's God who is driving the big rig. All we need to do is go old-school and keep our ears on. We need to tune in to the Holy Spirit and let Him speak through us.

When God gave us a new name, our new fancy handle, we agreed to let the Holy Spirit become our new dispatcher. The Bible describes Him as "another Advocate" or "the Spirit of truth" (see John 14:16–17 NRSV) who lives in us and with us and around us. Can you sense His presence in your life? Can you sense His voice directing your steps?

Being the hands and feet of Christ is about showing up when someone is hurting. The Holy Spirit will take away our fears—our fear of rejection, our fear of not knowing what to say or how to help someone. Christ said, "You will receive power when the Holy Spirit comes on you; and you will be my witnesses in Jerusalem, and in all Judea and Samaria, and to the ends of the earth" (Acts 1:8).

It's time to put our ears on—and make it all about Him.

Lord, Jesus, I'm so thankful that in times of trouble—especially in those moments when everything and everyone seem too weird to handle—the Holy Spirit comes and carries me toward wholeness and peace. Help me stay tuned in. Amen.

# CHAPTER 18

# WITHSTANDING THE TEST OF TIME

*Indeed, the word of God is living and active, sharper than any two-edged sword, piercing until it divides soul from spirit, joints from marrow; it is able to judge the thoughts and intentions of the heart. And before him no creature is hidden, but all are naked and laid bare to the eyes of the one to whom we must render an account.*

HEBREWS 4:12–13 NRSV

My very first horse saddle was made for a full-grown man. My grandpa Smokey gave it to me when he bought me my first horse, Roanie. The saddle was solid with a rawhide pommel and cantle. It was both basic and awesome, and I loved that saddle. It was really heavy for a skinny twelve-year-old girl. But instead of complaining, I found ways to adapt.

When it was time to saddle my fifteen-hand horse, I would begin by tying her to the pole of our basketball hoop. Then I would pull the four-wheeler up next to her, stand on the seat, lift the heavy saddle up onto her back, cinch up my gear, and climb on top. Roanie was the most patient horse I've ever known.

I am truly thankful for my grandpa and that amazing horse he gave me. I kept that saddle for most of my life. I had the opportunity to pass it along to a friend about five years ago. At that time, I had a cowboy out

of Oregon make me a new one that is a lot easier for me to maneuver. He even printed my favorite Bible verse (1 Peter 5:7) onto the leather on the back.

As I was shopping for a new saddle, I began to think about how some things change more than others. Other items—like my old saddle—withstand the test of time. I grew up with it and used it as an adult. Today, I own that saddle again, and now my kids are enjoying it too.

The Scriptures have also stood the test of time. They have been written, copied, spoken, shared, and translated time and time again. And God still continues to use these words to speak His love into the world. Even when the passages seem hard to comprehend, we have been given so many resources to help us connect with God through His Word. And when we gain insight, we can turn around and share that with others and help them understand too.

I've been there. I remember a time when I was really struggling to read my Bible. I was so curious and wanted to know about Jesus, but I didn't know where to start. One night, backstage at one of my husband's tour stops, I asked comedian Reno Collier for help. (Reno was the opening act for Dan's show—*Larry the Cable Guy*.) I'm so glad he didn't blow me off and say, "Just read your Bible." I would have been very discouraged. Instead, Reno gave me a book that simplified the New Testament that helped me so much. He had gotten it from his church, and even though it was out of print, he passed it along to me. It was a great way to start.

> The Scriptures have . . . stood the test of time.

Slowly I began to understand my need for a Savior and how these Scriptures applied directly to my life. With time I grew spiritually, and I eventually began to enjoy reading several different versions or translations of the Word. Along the way I have discovered study Bibles, reputable websites, social media pages, phone apps, and books that have helped me grow. But I still have the book Reno gave me that night.

God's Word has been so instrumental in my spiritual life that I love to share it with others. I have handed out hundreds of Bibles to people, and I intend to continue to do so. But I also understand that for the folks who are just beginning their journey toward Christ, these extra tools can be very helpful. For example, I share my favorite Bible app with people all the time. Sometimes I help them download it and get started on the spot.

Anyone who is earnestly searching for God will find Him. And anyone who honestly desires to study the Scriptures will discover all that the Bible has to offer. Sometimes their path to the Word is through the use of another platform like a good devotional, podcast, or app. Remember, "The word of God is alive and active. Sharper than any double-edged sword, it penetrates even to dividing soul and spirit, joints and marrow; it judges the thoughts and attitudes of the heart." God's Word has stood the test of time, and it always will—no matter what format it comes in.

......................................................................................

Lord, thank You for these sixty-six love letters You have given us in the sixty-six books of the Bible. I know the Bible is far from irrelevant, and I know that getting scriptural truths from my head to my heart (and eventually into my feet) can result in amazing, unexplainable changes that will transform the way I think, love, live, and serve. Transform my life through Your living Word. Amen.

# CHAPTER 19

# THE CONE OF SHAME

*I pray that you may have the power to comprehend,*
*with all the saints, what is the breadth and length*
*and height and depth, and to know the love of*
*Christ that surpasses knowledge, so that you*
*may be filled with all the fullness of God.*
EPHESIANS 3:18–19 NRSV

At some point in the life of nearly every dog and cat, our furry friend will end up wearing a "cone of shame." You know what I'm talking about: those awkward plastic cylinders that look like Elizabethan collars. I understand the need for them. A cone keeps your pet from scratching or licking a fresh wound, giving it time to heal. It's often called the "cone of shame" because of the look you get from your pet when it has to wear one. Its weighty eyes stare at you with a look of sadness. Even though pets don't wear these as a form of punishment, their seemingly guilty eyes stare up at you through the truncated cone—shame written all over their faces.

Recently one of our dogs had to get a growth removed from her eyelid.

She came home wearing the cone of shame, and I was instructed to leave it on her until the wound healed. It really was the best way to keep her from scratching at her eyelid, yet I'm not sure who it was harder for—the dog or me. I took it off as often as I could, until she started scratching her wound and I had to put it back on. I loathe the cone of shame because I feel like it makes my dog think she's failed me in some way. I can't stand the thought of that.

> I loathe the cone of shame because I feel like it makes my dog think she's failed me in some way.

There is a difference between guilt and shame. Guilt is knowing you have done something wrong and feeling sorry for it. It's a heavy emotion that points out a shortcoming or failure. It can also prompt you to own your mistakes and seek out ways to make amends. Shame takes things to the next level. It's when you grab onto your guilt and believe that you are a bad person. Your shortcomings actually become part of your identity. Guilt and shame go together sometimes. But they can also exist separately in your life. Defining ourselves through shame keeps us from growing in Christ. It pulls us away from embracing our true identities as children of God. And when we are not growing in Christ, it's really hard to share God's love and forgiveness with others.

The moment we ask for forgiveness, God forgives. Unfortunately, there are a lot of Christians who don't really believe this is true. Some folks have a very fearful view of God. They believe they have to keep asking for forgiveness for the same sin over and over again. They have a hard time accepting God's grace. Being caught up in emotions of guilt can be

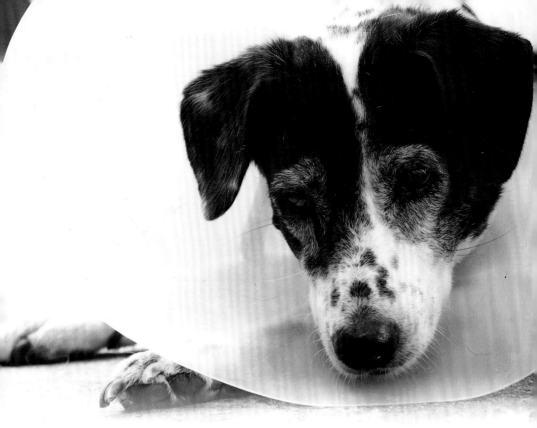

very discouraging and make us feel distant from God. But God is right there with us all the time, looking at us with compassion and tenderness. Even in those moments when you least expect God to forgive, He will reach out with grace. You are forgiven, period.

We live in a real world. Even when God forgives, sometimes other people don't. We fear that if our past mistakes are revealed, it would change other people's perceptions of us—especially when we make the decision to identify as a Christian. It feels like there are some people who are just waiting in the wings to point out all the bad things we have ever done in our lives. It's like we are being vetted for political office or something. It took me about a year to get over the fear of my past being exposed if I spoke in boldness for Christ. Then I got some great advice from my friend Dr. Arnie Cole, who said, "Don't worry about it."

It was that straightforward advice that helped me say, "I'm not going to worry about that." So I decided to stop using that cone of shame to bury my head. Instead, I'm going to use it as a megaphone (since it's already shaped like one) to witness about the saving power of Jesus. As my husband says, "There are things I look back on, and I wish I really wouldn't have done. I know there are some people who won't forgive me. But I know that Jesus does."

Can you relate? Do you sometimes struggle with guilt, maybe even shame, over past sins? The truth is, we all do. Yet a shame-filled mind is the Devil's playground. Embarrassment and regret can be a tiring distraction. They can pull me away from my true identity. I am honestly sorry for some of the things I have done. But I now live in the truth that I am forgiven. I am not going to let my regret of past mistakes slow me down from telling others about Christ's love. I am encouraged when I read my Bible and discover so many people who have also dealt with guilt and shame whom God used in amazing ways. God is bigger than anything we have done or any thought we have had.

Despite our sinfulness, despite our shortcomings, despite the high opinions that we hold of ourselves, we are still a part of God's bigger mission for the world. The words that flow from our forgiven souls carry life to a dying world. So excuse me a minute while I straighten my cone!

......................................................................

Lord, help me know "the love of Christ that surpasses knowledge." I want to be filled with all the fullness of God. Deliver me from fear and shame. Heal my identity. Amen.

# CHAPTER 20

# I'M A PRODIGAL TOO

*"'My son,' the father said, 'you are always with me,*
*and everything I have is yours. But we had to celebrate*
*and be glad, because this brother of yours was dead*
*and is alive again; he was lost and is found.'"*

<small>LUKE 15:31–32</small>

Our heavenly Father never leaves things as they are. He's always at work, creating, perfecting, regenerating—reclaiming what's His. That includes us.

God knows our stubborn hearts, our thoughts, our hang-ups—our past. And yet He never gives up on us. Instead, He goes one step further and gives us so much more than we deserve!

Barbara, a horse-loving single mom who lives on a ranch in Boise, Idaho, simply could not comprehend this truth. She had given her life to Christ years ago, yet she still couldn't believe that Jesus had forgiven her. Just like you and me, Barbara is a prodigal. Let me share her story.

Barbara regretted so many decisions and actions from her younger years: racking up so much debt she and her family could barely make ends meet, eventual divorce that all but crushed her daughter's heart, more out-of-control spending, putting her own needs first, coveting, worrying. *Stupid*, Barbara thought to herself. *I did a bunch of stupid things as a young woman. I lived in darkness, wasting precious time.*

But even after she had prayed and committed her life to Jesus, Barbara simply couldn't let go of the past. Day after day she hobbled along spiritually as if her heart were in shackles. And for more than a decade she hid behind a mask, letting the world see a tough woman, an unbreakable wife and mother. But on the inside, she was grieving—beating herself up, constantly feeling immobilized and neutralized by fear, worry, and doubt.

One day, right in the middle of her muddy backyard, something remarkable happened: Barbara came clean with Christ. She found the

courage to release every festering memory, to surrender every vile choice.

> Even after she had prayed and committed her life to Jesus, Barbara simply couldn't let go of the past.

It was a mundane chore, but just as she had always done, day in, day out, she walked around her backyard, watering trees, shrubs, grass, even the bare ground her dogs had trampled. As she tugged on the hose, moving it in a rhythmic, mechanical motion, drenching every pebble and clump of dirt, her mind began to flood with thought after thought—mostly painful ones.

*Child of God? Christ-follower? Liar. That's who I really am.*

She took a few more steps and sprayed the center of her yard. *Fool—that's what I am. Forgiven? How can I ever be forgiven for my stupidity—my lack of common sense?!*

"Let it go."

Barbara froze in her tracks and looked around.

"*Release it.*"

She nearly dropped the hose. God had her attention. She sensed Him nudging her heart, extending a hand that would pull her out of her emotional pit.

"*Trust Me.*"

But Barbara was afraid to take His hand. *I can't, Lord. I simply can't. I'm the "captain of my ship, the master of my destiny" as they say. I know right from wrong, and I made all those stupid choices. That's why I simply—*

"*No, Barbara. This is wrong! I am God, and I have forgiven you. But you haven't forgiven yourself.*"

This time she dropped the hose and broke into tears.

There she stood—alone with her Creator. Water gushing every-where, puddles rising in the mud, and tears rolling down her cheeks. And then she began to laugh and cry all at the same time.

*Yes—You are right!*

Barbara paused and considered carefully the truth that was staring her in the face. *Yes—I really haven't forgiven myself. Yet, Lord, I now see that You have. I can let go. I am free!*

Barbara felt like jumping and dancing in the mud. She wanted to scream from the top of her lungs: "Thank You, God! I get it now. Thank You, thank You!"

Suddenly, the cross made much more sense. Salvation through Christ—her redemption—was real! Even though she had beaten herself up day after day, her Savior had been mending all those broken pieces, destroying the mask, releasing her from the shackles, and wiping away the flowing tears.

Barbara is a prodigal—just like you and me. She was once lost and alone, yet because God loves her and pursues her—something that she can't begin to comprehend—all she can do is thank Him.

> Barbara is a prodigal—just like you and me.

Even now as a mature Christ-follower, Barbara knows she still doesn't have it all together. Just when she thinks she has finally mastered a doubt and a struggle in her life, another issue pops up. Before she knows it, she's fretting again. First it's an excessive preoccupation with life's uncer-tainties, then constant what-if thoughts that seem to stab at her stomach, then panic—even anger.

*Is this just how it is in life?*

That day as she stood in her backyard, she took a deep breath and pictured the faces of her family—from the perfect smile of her beautiful daughter (now married with her own kids) to her sweet ninety-two-year-old mother who now needs her care. Even her "zoo" of scruffy pets soothed her heart.

Barbara slipped back into her house—ready to end another routine day. She knew that the next day would bring a new batch of challenges. "In this world we will have trouble," she reminded herself. "But take heart! I have overcome the world," Jesus promised (John 16:33).

We must never forget the scandalous amount of grace God extends to us. Grace reminds us that we are the prodigal son. We are reminded about loss, about the mistakes we made, and all the roads we chose that led us to ruin and heartache. If we forget about the grace of God, we start to live our faith like the prodigal's older brother in the Bible. He had no idea that his father didn't want his obedience or his service. His father just wanted his love and for him to be in a relationship with him. (For the full story, see Luke 15:11–31.)

The older brother reminds me of all the things that are required of me to care for my family physically, like feed them, fold their clothes, and drive them to their appointments on time. But how much further can I reveal my love to them through relationship by giving them a hug, asking them about their day, and ignoring that sink full of dirty dishes so I can spend time with them cuddling on the couch?

...........................................................................................................

Lord, thank You for my home, my family, my life—my little bit of heaven on earth. Thank You for Your grace. You forgive and then give so much back. Help me to trust more, to change what needs to be changed, to grow, and to serve You. Amen.

# CHAPTER 21

# JUST LEAVE THE LIGHT ON

*Your teachings are wonderful,*
*and I respect them all.*
*Understanding your word*
*brings light*
*to the minds*
*of ordinary people.*
*I honestly want to know*
*everything you teach.*
Psalm 119:129–131 cev

I always get a kick out of those folksy Motel 6 commercials, which have buzzed the airwaves for as long as I can remember—and to this day are still going strong! Right after the quirky music kicks in, that always-friendly, ever-familiar voice delivers a slogan that's as American as apple pie: "I'm Tom Bodett for Motel 6, and we'll leave the light on for you."

As a horse-loving girl who grew up in Wisconsin, I was inspired by those commercials to take a road trip somewhere—*anywhere!* I'd study a map and dream up all kinds of possibilities: *Maybe we'll drive West to the Grand Canyon . . . and then on to Disneyland. Maybe we'll head up the coast to the Golden Gate Bridge and ride a cable car!*

But because my dad needed to stay close to the milk cows, reality was much less impressive: the Museum of Woodcarving in Shell Lake, the Freshwater Fishing Hall of Fame in Hayward, Al Capone's Hideout in Couderay. If we were lucky, we'd take a long drive to Lake Superior, with a pit stop at the SS *Meteor* Whaleback Ship Museum! Still, I wasn't picky. I loved road trips.

As an adult, Tom's famous phrase makes me think far less about traveling and much more about *sharing*. Leaving the light on is a simple way to care for somebody.

When I physically (or symbolically) leave the light on, it's as if I'm welcoming someone in. I'm bringing them out of the cold and the darkness of this world, and I'm attending to their needs. It's a basic way to minister to someone—even if it's for just a little while.

And in everyday life, we can leave the light on in so many different ways:

- giving away a little kindness to those around us
- encouraging a stranger
- serving a neighbor
- looking someone in the eye and asking how their day is going
- paying an honest compliment
- loving the lost

Most of all, leaving the light on enables me to introduce others to the God I know and trust. For example, I used to think that if I studied

Scripture long and hard, I'd discover the silver bullet—that all-powerful verse that would help me "win" an unbelieving heart. I meant well. I sincerely have a heart for those who don't know Jesus—especially unbelieving family and friends. One friend I know believes in the "possibility of God," but he just won't commit to a relationship with Jesus. He also doesn't think there's only one path to heaven. I've had hours of conversations with him about sin, God, and salvation, but my friend just won't budge. I felt defeated and in turmoil for my lost friend. And then I met a pastor with more than forty years of experience who felt equally defeated. He was unable to persuade a terminally ill man to make a commitment to Christ. Here's what he learned: Jesus does the saving, not us. There is no silver bullet, magic formula, or argument that can persuade someone to hand their life over to God. That's because it's a heart issue. Each one of us must have a personal encounter with Jesus, and then He gives us the freedom to choose.

It's been a few years since the last spiritual conversation I had with my friend, and since I simply left my light on, he has recently started to open back up to me again. But this time, instead of trying to blind him with bright spiritual platitudes, I listen. It has not been without difficultly, but let's just say I learned the hard way that I needed to replace my evangelist bulb with an LED bulb. Because sometimes I may need to leave a light on for a very long time. And this is where I've had to grow spiritually and trust in the character of God, who, more than me, does not wish for any of us to perish. Not even the real stinkers of this world. I know this firsthand, because you know what? I used to be one of them.

> There is no silver bullet, magic formula, or argument that can persuade someone to hand their life over to God.

Let's just say I learned the hard way that I needed to replace my evangelist bulb with an LED bulb.

Through the ages, the nature and character of God have been described in countless ways—holy, compassionate, merciful, gracious, loving, faithful, forgiving, just to name a few. Yet He has one very special character trait that everybody can relate to: He is *giving* (James 1:5).

We have life only because God has created us by an exercise of His will. We can receive salvation because He wills to grant it. God's ever-giving heart allows us to approach Him.

God is the infinite, holy Creator who has always existed and who made the universe by the power of His command (Hebrews 11:3). God told Moses, "I am who I am" (Exodus 3:14). There is only one true God (Isaiah 45:5). He is the sovereign Lord, the God of Scripture, who acts in His creation and who involves Himself intimately in our lives.

God is the Shepherd who guides (Genesis 48:15), the Lord who provides (Genesis 22:8), the Lord of peace during life's trials (Judges 6:24), the Physician who heals the sick (Exodus 15:26), and the Banner that guides the soldier (Exodus 17:8–16).

God is the Alpha and the Omega: the beginning and the end (Revelation 1:8).
God is Immanuel: "God with us" (Isaiah 7:14).
God is our Father (Isaiah 9:6).
God is holy (1 Samuel 2:2).
God is love (1 John 4:16).

Yet our giving Creator won't force us into a relationship with Him. He simply loves us too much, so He gives us the freedom to choose. Author Max Lucado explains it this way:

> God will whisper. He will shout. He will touch and tug. He will take away our burdens; He'll even take away our blessings. If there are a thousand steps between us and Him, He will take all but one. But He will leave the final one for us. The choice is ours.[1]

But the Lord does want us to make the introduction.

That's where leaving the light on comes into play. Everyone who knows me can pretty much figure out where I stand with Jesus. As I love, serve, and connect, they get a glimpse into my heart and see what compels it. They encounter light inside. And I choose to leave the light on.

................................................................................

Lord, please open my eyes to those around me. Open my heart to include and love those I encounter every day. Help me be a part of Your mission of love and restoration. Amen.

CHAPTER 22

# BARKING DOGS

*This is how we know what love is: Jesus Christ laid down*
*his life for us. And we ought to lay down our lives for our*
*brothers and sisters. If anyone has material possessions and*
*sees a brother or sister in need but has no pity on them, how*
*can the love of God be in that person? Dear children, let us*
*not love with words or speech but with actions and in truth.*

1 JOHN 3:16–18

My husband is a great gift giver—but that hasn't always been the case For many years, he did his minimum-dude duty and would grab a bouquet of flowers from the grocery store, giving them as gifts during birthdays and holidays.

While I love flowers, sometimes giving and receiving them begins to feel robotic and expected. Here's what I consider to be the best gifts of all: when Dan does something as simple as folding clothes or running my errands for me. These simple acts of love speak volumes over anything he can buy me. These actions tell me I am loved and appreciated. They assure me that he is truly here for me, willing to lift some of my daily burdens. These kinds of gifts get my attention!

One Valentine's Day Dan totally blew my mind. He surprised me with a small manure spreader that I could pull behind my ATV. I absolutely love it! And most days you can find me in the horse pasture doing my "poop duty." This is also when I try to catch a little quiet time with God. Nobody else in my family seems to appreciate mucking stalls as much as I do. So family members who are otherwise exceptionally needy make themselves scarce when it comes time for that chore. Just me and God, my horses, and two dogs make up my barn party.

Just me and God, my horses, and two dogs make up my barn party.

Lately, though, I have been experiencing a disruption of my peace because my two rambunctious, easily excited companions absolutely, positively *will not stop barking*!

They bark at the manure spreader, at the donkeys, the birds—anything that moves or breathes. You name it. Barking tops my list of most aggravating sounds. As much as I love my dogs, I am gradually coming to the conclusion that they've got to stay at the house. (I'll plan a different activity they can participate in.)

My barking-dog dilemma has made me think a lot about how I share my faith. (By now you've probably figured out that just about everything makes me think about this!)

I've decided that I don't want to come off like a "barking dog" to those who don't yet know Christ. In other words, I want to avoid annoyingly spiritualizing everything every time I open my mouth. Discernment is a quality that we sometimes lack, and if we are going to be effective in communicating the truth, we need to do it with small actions that, over time, add up in big ways.

If a friend (let's call her Sue) was trying to set up another friend (we'll call her Ann) with a perfect man but constantly talked about how much of a loser Ann would be without this stranger in her life—not to mention that if Ann didn't marry him, she'd end up in hell—Ann would probably start avoiding Sue faster than a group text message.

But if Sue talked about a man she'd met who wanted to meet Ann—and that he was currently teaching Sue how to be a better version of herself—that would probably catch Ann's attention. And if Sue's actions toward Ann (and other people) proved that she was dependable, sincere, and selfless, I think Sue wouldn't have any problems being heard. She certainly wouldn't come across like a barking dog!

What I'm really talking about is communicating love that none of us can push away or hide from—love that grows and blooms.

I don't have the stats, but I would imagine we tend to bark too much at our close friends and relatives. Why? Because we love them so much. And since they love us too, they usually try to tolerate it. But no matter how much I love my dogs, if they keep barking incessantly, I will start to tune them out, and then eventually they are no longer going to get an invite to the barn party.

God is continuously courting unbelievers in ways we don't know, yet He includes us in the courtship by prompting us to do a little wooing on His behalf too. So one of the best ways to show Jesus to others is in the details.

> I don't have the stats, but I would imagine we tend to bark too much at our close friends and relatives.

If you've shared your faith with someone, yet they don't seem too receptive, don't be discouraged. Let God do the saving, and continue being you—without barking on and on about it. Occasionally God may prompt you to fill a need for them, send them a random text message of encouragement, or—yes—maybe even send them flowers. These actions tell them they are loved and appreciated, and it communicates that you are there for them—willing to lift some of their daily burden.

Whichever way you are called to serve, make sure you are ready to execute God's prompting; this way you will make the gospel seem that much more attractive.

Lord, help me choose my words carefully when I share my faith. Help me be tender, loving, and compassionate toward others. Let others see You through my words and actions. Amen.

CHAPTER 23

# BLOOD, SWEAT, TEARS, AND TIME

*Two are better than one,*
*because they have a good return for their labor:*
*If either of them falls down,*
*one can help the other up.*
*But pity anyone who falls*
*and has no one to help them up.*
*Also, if two lie down together, they will keep warm.*
*But how can one keep warm alone?*
*Though one may be overpowered,*
*two can defend themselves.*
*A cord of three strands is not quickly broken.*

ECCLESIASTES 4:9–12

*I* couldn't help breaking into a victory dance—right in the middle of my kitchen, with pots boiling, the blender buzzing, and the microwave timer threatening "T-minus ten seconds to total food annihilation."

My friend Tracy sent me some much-needed encouragement through a simple text message, so I had to stop what I was doing, delay dinner, and soak in every amazing word.

And the more I read, the more I danced!

> The more I read, the more I danced!

In her text, she told how she used a piece of art to share her faith with a total stranger. During a random conversation with another woman, Tracy sensed the Lord nudging her to talk about a painting she owns—and the story behind it. But here's the cool part: the artwork Tracy used had been created by my sister Jody!

My home in Nebraska is filled with Jody's paintings—everything from landscapes to portraits. Jody is an accomplished artist whose paintings entice the eyes and stir the emotions. One of them is called "The Woman at the Well," and that's the painting Tracy used to talk about God. The artwork is based on a passage of Scripture in John 4:1–26, which tells the story of Jesus meeting a Samaritan woman as she draws water from a well. This was scandalous in Jesus' day. But He spoke with her anyway. And after asking her for a drink, He shared with the woman the way to eternal life: "Everyone who drinks this water will be thirsty again, but whoever drinks the water I give them will never thirst. Indeed, the water I give them will become in them a spring of water welling up to eternal life" (vv. 13–14).

As Tracy told the story behind the painting, she explained how Jesus came to save every man, woman, and child on the face of the planet. "God

loves everybody," she explained, "and He doesn't want anyone to miss spending eternity with Him. That's what Jesus was sharing at the well."

After rereading the text, and dancing around a little more, I forwarded Tracy's message to Jody. *She's going to love this more than me.*

Tracy's story was perfectly timed, and as it turns out, my sister Jody was in great need of some encouragement too. Later Jody told me, "Sometimes I've wondered if I'm wasting my time and energy where I shouldn't be." But hearing how our friend Tracy had used Jody's art for God changed everything for her.

Like I said, the timing was perfect. Or to be more precise, *God's timing was perfect.*

*God's timing was perfect.* The stranger, my sister, and I were each filled with joy because Tracy followed a tug in her heart. Here's something else my friend had shown me: "Two are better than one, because they have a good return for their labor" (Ecclesiastes 4:9). In other words, we're in this together.

It's a gathering of saints and sinners, arm in arm, holding each other up. It's a growing community of Christ-followers who have joined together—crying and laughing with each other, praying, serving, and straining toward God, step by step, day by day.

I'm so thankful we share this journey with our friends and family as we strive to share the good news. And it's a relief knowing we aren't expected to do it alone. Gospel proclaimers are only human, and we're not physically or spiritually bulletproof. This is another reason Jesus sent His disciples out into the world "two by two" (Mark 6:7). In fact, the use of pairs for preaching and serving continues throughout the book of Acts (see 13:1–3 and 15:39–41).

We each share a part in the delivery of God's awesome, life-saving message—but just one part. So we shouldn't feel discouraged when we don't see results, and we shouldn't ever feel that we're wasting our time. The truth is, we may never see how our part fits into the big picture, especially when it often takes two people to plant a seed and another three to water it. But that's what it's all about: caring, sharing, and doing life together. As we combine our strengths, creativity, talents, and ambitions, we can accomplish more on God's behalf than if we ever tried to go at it alone.

Go ahead—get down on your knees right now and thank God for the Tracys in your life: friends who pray for you and offer spiritual encouragement. "Two can defend themselves. A cord of three strands is not quickly broken."

Lord, thank You that we never have to go it alone. Thank You for the part You've given me and the part You've given my friends and family as we go and make disciples. Help us support each other and seek Your direction as we care, share, and do life together. Amen.

CHAPTER 24

# DON'T WASTE YOUR WELTS

*We gladly suffer, because we know that suffering*
*helps us to endure. And endurance builds character,*
*which gives us a hope that will never disappoint us.*
*All of this happens because God has given us the*
*Holy Spirit, who fills our hearts with his love.*

ROMANS 5:3–5 CEV

I am so bummed. Apparently, the older I get, the more allergic to horses I become. Horse dander has always given me red, itchy eyes. But lately it is also giving me red, itchy welts. Recently a woman learned of my horse allergy by reading my book *Unbridled Faith*. She asked, "Do you see another lesson here? Maybe you're learning to follow your dreams even when there are bumps in the road."

I had to ponder her question for a bit. For me, it's more about how Jesus is always with me even when life is hard. It's a reminder that while this world is important, so is our eternity. Someday I will be in my permanent home—heaven. I'm not sure if horses will be there, but if they are, I can imagine running with ease though the grassy meadow with Shetland ponies. Here on earth, I'm overweight, I can't run, I break out in hives, and Shetland ponies are ornery. But I live here, right now, in the reality of this world, and sometimes it's not easy. Don't believe it if anyone tells you that following Jesus will make your life easier or make you rich or healthier. Jesus says we will have trials (John 16:33), so go ahead and expect them. Make no mistake, I want to encourage you to follow your dreams despite the bumps in the road. Work hard toward your goals. But just know that God may have a different plan for you. Life often takes unexpected turns. This was made perfectly clear to me over the last eleven months as I watched my friend Ann navigate life after her twelve-year-old son, Christian, was diagnosed with cancer. It was so unfair that he was faced with stage-four cancer at such a young age. But Jesus was right there with them.

The difficult moments in life make us stronger. We can learn so much from facing our worst fears. The welts of life are real, and they hurt sometimes. Even when it seems unbearable, there is always hope. I have more faith than ever before because I know that God is good. His promises are true, and He is for us. I still have questions as to why Christian had to be called home so soon, but it doesn't make me question God's goodness. Even when my fervent prayers were not answered the way I longed for, it was vital to keep the faith.

> The difficult moments in life make us stronger.

Prayer helps to align our hearts with God's heart. The objective should always be to open ourselves up to Him and be molded into His ways. As this relationship grows, we can find peace even when we don't understand the "why." Through our struggles we not only grow but are able to have more compassion for others.

At Christian's funeral service, Ann reassuringly told us, "I can be okay, even when I have overwhelming feelings." I can be okay, even if . . . fill in the blank. In that moment Ann showed us how God's grace and strength are sufficient. Ann is going to be okay, and we will be okay too. What a powerful message and a powerful witness for Jesus.

I thought I had a handle on this until about six years ago when I had my own cancer scare. Although it was terrifying, it ended up being a good thing for my faith, kind of a cherry on the top of it. During this health scare I discovered that caring for other people was an important part of living the Christian life. Even though my health scare turned out well, I am thankful that I was able to grow closer to God with a renewed hope for the future and passion to share the good news. I have not forgotten that my life's purpose is to tell others that Jesus is our only hope against the inevitable welts of this world.

Lord, suffering is hard—so please give me the strength, peace, hope, and joy I need to endure. But more than anything, help me never waste my welts. Use my struggles to bring glory to You. Amen.

# CHAPTER 25

# HELL FOR COWS

*He will punish those who do not know God and do not*
*obey the gospel of our Lord Jesus. They will be punished*
*with everlasting destruction and shut out from the*
*presence of the Lord and from the glory of his might.*

2 THESSALONIANS 1:8–9

L et's talk cow tipping for a minute. Because unless you know something about it, you really don't know anything about it.

We've all heard of people who claim to have actually tipped cows over.
Sorry to disappoint you, but I'm going to bust that myth. The truth is, cow
tipping is just an urban legend.

I know a thing or two about cows, and I know that cow tipping is
impossible. And I know a thing or two about urban legends: stories that
are circulated around as true, that have supposedly happened to a friend
or family member, and that can be humorous or horrifying. Like people
who claim they have been cow tipping, or have found a hook on their car
door handle, or who have come in contact with a vanishing hitchhiker.

And even though these urban legends are not true, they do reveal important truths about our deepest, darkest fears or our need for attention. I wonder if hell for cows is knowing there are humans in the world who think they can knock them over. (No, wait—I'm pretty sure it's the fear of becoming a flame-licked patty.)

I wonder if hell for cows is knowing there are humans in the world who think they can knock them over.

But on a serious note, for some things in life, we need to know if they are true or fictitious—like heaven and hell. It seems as if way more people believe in the existence of heaven than hell. Some people treat hell as if it were some kind of urban legend rather than a real place. According to the Bible, both places are very real. It's a hard topic to think about. And it's an even harder subject to discuss with others. But there are a lot of people who earnestly want to know if these two destinations really exist and how they end up in one or the other. Since I sincerely care about people, I want everyone to be in heaven. I can't stand the idea of anyone spending eternity in a place of torment.

Jesus came to earth and made the ultimate sacrifice so we can all be forgiven and spend eternity in the presence of God. I have a great sadness when I hear of someone passing away who had no faith or relationship with Christ. It is literally stressful for me. It doesn't matter what a person has done in their life; I do not want hell for them. I really don't. But as C. S. Lewis says, "I willingly believe that the damned are, in one sense, successful, rebels to the end; that the gates of hell are locked on the inside."[1] It is a personal decision for people to choose the freedom they are offered in Christ, or to shut the door to their soul and reject God. By choosing to reject God now, they are shutting the door from within when all they have to do is open up to Christ and embrace an eternity of freedom and celebration.

I praise God because I know that even though things get hard here on earth, we will be rejoicing when we get to the other side. Jesus taught us to pray, *Your kingdom come, here on earth as it is in heaven.* We get a little taste of heaven here and now. But we have so much to look forward to in our future. I imagine that getting to heaven is going to be like getting home from the worst trip of my life. There will be so much relief when I finally get to walk through the door of my house. My burdens will be gone, and all my baggage will be cast aside. It will be new and familiar at the same time. I will feel safe and comfortable. And I will be able to celebrate in the presence of God for eternity. I'm sure that my imagination doesn't even come close to the realities of heaven. I also imagine that hell will be the opposite. It will be an eternity that is absent of God's presence. No hope. No rest. No safety.

Having real conversations about heaven and hell is important. As we read our Bibles, we see the ongoing story of God loving us enough to offer us salvation instead of death. Jesus made His sacrifice on the cross so we could be in God's family and spend eternity with Him. If we believe, we cannot avoid the difficult topics like heaven and hell. People need to know that there is a path to heaven. And there is a path that leads away from God. The consequences of both of those paths are very real. It's not an urban legend. It's not a made-up story—like cow tipping. So share the good news. Let's help each other accept the forgiveness of Christ and live an eternity of praise and celebration.

> I imagine that getting to heaven is going to be like getting home from the worst trip of my life.

Lord, Your love is something we can't quite grasp. Yet because of it, You have forgiven our sin through Jesus Christ and graciously brought us back into fellowship. Abandoning Your unholy, imperfect children is unthinkable to You. We have eternal life through You! Amen.

# CHAPTER 26

# SWAPPING STORIES: MINE, YOURS, GOD'S

*"The people dwelling in darkness
have seen a great light,
and for those dwelling in the region and shadow of death,
on them a light has dawned."*

MATTHEW 4:16 ESV

A s Stephanie spoke, she could see the kids' eyes growing wider and wider, and the little wheels spinning inside their heads. The young teacher finally had her students' attention.

"Danger was encroaching," she continued, "but the man was clueless." Stephanie gestured with her hands, moved her legs, and used her whole body to act out the scenes. "All of a sudden—and as if from out of nowhere—robbers attacked. They beat the man, and then they tossed him on the ground, leaving him hurt and alone. Blood was everywhere."

The children gasped.

Her retelling of the parable of the good Samaritan (from Luke 10:25–37) was getting through to her otherwise squirrely third graders. Now it was time to pull them into the drama. "Suddenly, a priest happened to be going down that same road. Do you know what happened next?"

Hands shot up. "He stopped and helped," someone blurted.

Stephanie shook her head no. "When he saw the man, he passed by on the other side. Can you believe it? And then a Levite came along, but he passed by on the other side too. But a Samaritan came to the place where the man was. When he saw the man, what do you suppose he did?"

"He ran away too," a boy yelled.

"No," a girl chimed in. "He was good, and he tried to help."

"That's right," Stephanie agreed. "He felt sorry for the guy, so he went to him, poured olive oil and wine on his wounds, and bandaged them. Then he put the man on his own donkey. He brought him to an inn and took care of him. The next day he took out two silver coins. He gave them to the owner of the inn. 'Take care of him,' he said. 'When I return, I will pay you back for any extra expense you may have.'"

The teacher paused and looked a student in the eye. "Which of the

three do you think was a good neighbor to the man who was attacked by robbers?"

"The Samaritan," he responded.

"That's right," Stephanie said with a smile. "He was the only one who had compassion for the man. And Jesus tells us, 'Go and do as he did.'"

Parables have a way capturing our imaginations and teaching profound spiritual lessons—and they're as effective on adults as they are on little kids. In the Gospels, Jesus used them on everyone from burly Roman soldiers to timid children. I use them too.

A parable is a story about a simple, everyday subject that can illustrate a deeper moral truth. The word *parable* means "a placement side by side for the purpose of comparison."[1] For example, in the story about the good Samaritan, Jesus used a scene from the tumultuous region to teach the importance of looking out for each other—even showing love and mercy. (By the way, there are twenty-three parables in Matthew, eight in Mark, and twenty-four in Luke.)

We can use parables to disciple young believers and to share our faith with those who don't know God at all. But in order to "communicate Christ" effectively, some key things need to happen.

1. *Avoid Christianese and theo-babble.* When I was in my twenties, a well-meaning Christian told me that I was a sinner and that I needed to repent. But since I grew up with zero religion in my life, I had no clue what people were saying to me. "Lost sheep?" "Repent?" "Saved by the blood of the lamb?" "Limited atonement

or justification?" "Monergism or synergism?" "Moner-syner-limited-but-irresistible". . . What?!

2. *Make it personal, and share from the heart.* That's what Jesus did. He was the master at having a good conversation, being honest, being compassionate, and serving others. That's why He wove parables into conversations. As I look back, I realize that if someone had communicated a parable in a way I could have related to, it would have helped me understand that the "Son of Man" came so none of His "lost sheep" should perish. Eventually, I learned that the sheep are you and me and that He loves us with a fierce passion. It's that passion that has inspired me to go into the world and make disciples.

3. *Swap a few stories—mine, yours, God's.* In other words, let people see who you are inside—what you're all about, what shapes you, what you believe. Relate your story to theirs and then connect it to God's (creation, salvation, redemption, hope). "But make sure that in your hearts you honor Christ as Lord. Always be ready to give an answer to anyone who asks you about the hope you have. Be ready to give the reason for it. But do it gently and with respect" (1 Peter 3:15 NIRV).

4. *Don't neglect the "happy sinners."* For years, I didn't have a relationship with Jesus, yet I was happy. I was in great health, I was charitable, I was in a great relationship, and I had a great job. Too often Christians get this idea that the only people we need to share with are addicts or the homeless. While the situation is dire for broken people, it isn't any more dire than the soul of a person who thinks he or she has it all together. We're all broken.

The truth is, we all need Christ. And here's our hope: "He has made everything beautiful in its time. He has also set eternity in the human heart; yet no one can fathom what God has done from beginning to end" (Ecclesiastes 3:11). Because of this, it didn't matter how good things were going in my life before Christ. This "eternity" made me wrestle internally with questions I had about God and whether there was a purpose for my life.

Statistically, I should not even be a believer. Research from lots of smart people at various universities—including organizations like Barna and the National Association of Evangelicals (NAE)—come to the same conclusion: 97 percent of individuals become Christians *before* the age of thirty, and only 3 out of 100 after that age.[2] But God's promises *are* true, and we need to rely on the fact that He makes all human hearts stir to know Him. Today my life goal is to disappoint the Enemy by going into all the world and making disciples—even the "happy ones."

While we may be among the ninety-nine who are safe in the sheep pen (see Luke 15:3–7), imagine the joy in heaven when we're able to add one more.

.........................................................................

Lord, thank You for setting eternity in my heart. Help me always be ready to give an answer for the hope I have in You. Give me the honor of "adding one more." Amen.

# CHAPTER 27

# IT AIN'T ABOUT ME

*For this is what the Lord has commanded us: "I
have made you a light for the Gentiles, that you
may bring salvation to the ends of the earth."*
ACTS 13:47

As my family and I were packing and preparing to return home from
a trip to Arizona, my golf-crazed husband and a buddy of his just
had to get in one last round. Honestly, if they had the opportunity, I think
they'd play golf all the way to the airport, at the airport, on the plane, in
baggage claim, even in the restroom! For most serious golfers, that's par
for the course, right? Yet before they could even set foot on the greens and
tee up, their plans came to a screeching halt. Dan's friend received one of
those phone calls everyone dreads—the kind that usually comes in the
wee hours of the morning when your mind is full of cobwebs.

He punched the off button on his cell phone and looked my husband
in the eye. "I've got to get home to Chicago right away," he said. "It's my
mom. It doesn't look good. They just put her in hospice care."

Dan's heart sank. "Absolutely," he said without hesitation. "Let's get you home."

Time was precious, and Dan knew we had to act fast. But to make matters worse, a snowstorm was barreling toward the Midwest. Could his friend get back to Chicago in time to console his mom—and ultimately say goodbye?

We all know the frustrations and uncertainties of air travel. Things can really go awry when the Lord lets a blizzard swallow up the skies. My mind immediately flashed to the movie *Planes, Trains, and Automobiles*. With no desire to see our hurting friend stranded or forced to share a motel room with a sweaty man who sells shower curtain rings, we decided to put him on a private flight. And because tragedy can open a window to share Christ and be a comfort, we knew we had to make the trip with him.

> Could his friend get back to Chicago in time to console his mom—and ultimately say goodbye?

After a mad dash to the airport, and then parking, loading luggage, and corralling the kids onto the plane, the engines soon roared, and we were climbing safely above the clouds. I immediately began praying for the right words and the perfect moment to witness. Yet without realizing it, "me, myself, and I" were quickly getting in the way. Instead of just being a good friend to Dan's buddy, I started making this stressful moment all about . . . well, *me*!

Midway through the flight, I unbuckled and stood up. *It's now or never*, I told myself. *A friend's salvation hangs in the balance. I can't miss this chance!*

I joined the guys, but before a single word rolled off my tongue, I noticed that our friend wasn't doing so well. As soon as Dan would mention his friend's mom, his buddy would choke up. Suddenly, "abort mission" sirens blared in my head. No opening for the gospel here. So, instead, I retreated to my seat.

*Ugh!* I hate writing these words. It's even harder reliving them. Yet as I look back, I see clearly what was happening at that moment. I should have stayed and listened to our friend talk about golf, baseball—anything! But nope. Instead, I started pouting. I went back to my seat, and at some point I must have dozed off. About twenty minutes later, I opened my eyes to the sound of my husband giving our friend the gospel. It was very humbling.

As I sat alone in my seat, I began to see that I was treating our friend more like a project to pounce on and less like a hurting person who was about to lose his mom. Earlier, I had asked God to give *me* the words so *I* could share them. I was putting the focus on myself when—the whole time—it should have been on the needs of our friend.

You could argue that my heart was in the right place, but if I'm being honest with you, that wasn't the case. You know those moments when you hear a sermon, and you identify something in yourself that's kind of ugly, and your eyes are suddenly opened to the fact that you need Jesus more than ever? Well, this was one of those moments. And as I sat in my God-given "time out" in the back of that plane, I began to see that my heart was not for our friend, not really, but more about me looking and feeling really good about myself. *Give me the words*, I had prayed, *so I can do this or that.* I lost sight of a man who was grieving his mom.

The gospel ain't about me—or you.

I am so thankful that God's ultimate goal is not to see any one of us perish. He looks for a humble heart to deliver His life-saving message, and He found one in my husband that day. God did exactly what I had wanted, but I realize that it wasn't exactly what I had asked.

The world says, "Greatness consists of how many you lead." But God wants greatness to consist of how many you serve. We serve God by tending to the lost. I served my friend well by getting him on a plane home, but I lost sight of why he needed one to begin with. As we witness, we must focus on the friendship and tend to the person's needs first. And then—if the opening is made available—quench their thirst with that good Living Water.

...................................................................................

Lord Jesus, help me get out of the way and serve You. Humble my heart. And in Your perfect time, show me how to lead my friends and neighbors to the Living Water. Amen.

# CHAPTER 28

# COME ON IN, FRIEND—
# THE FIRE'S HOT!

*Praise God, the Father of our Lord Jesus Christ!*
*The Father is a merciful God, who always gives us*
*comfort. He comforts us when we are in trouble, so*
*that we can share that same comfort with others in*
*trouble. We share in the terrible sufferings of Christ,*
*but also in the wonderful comfort he gives.*
2 CORINTHIANS 1:3–5 CEV

A few months ago, I started missing God. I know this sounds a little shocking to the ears, and it's even weirder to write these words, yet I couldn't help feeling as if I were going through some sort of strange spiritual funk. On the outside, I was going through the motions of being a Christian—so everything looked just fine. But the inside was different. I felt empty. I wasn't really connecting with God, and I wasn't hearing Him or sensing His presence.

I was in a desert.

I had never experienced this before, so I can tell you, the silence between God and me was deafening. None of this was stemming from anger or doubt, and I still spent time praying and reading God's Word. So what was going on? After some soul searching and more than a few sleepless nights, I'd come to an uncomfortable conclusion: I was feeling this way because, for the first time, I wasn't in any type of trial or tribulation.

This, too, sounds a little shocking to the ears. I'm not suggesting that we can be close to God only when we face a trial. The Lord is always there, and we can be close or far away from Him regardless of our circumstances—whether we face trials or feel peace. But for me, I had become a bit too sedate in my faith, and I found myself wandering through a desert.

> I had become a bit too sedate in my faith, and I found myself wandering through a desert.

So what was I supposed to do? I wasn't about to pray for some fiery furnace to stand in. At one point in my faith walk, I was told to never pray for things like this, especially patience, because God could end up giving me a trial that would drag on for all eternity. And I was nervous that if I prayed for closeness with God, I'd end up in a wheelchair or something.

Early in my faith, I began this weird habit of viewing God like He was a sort of genie who was trying to pull one over on me with prayer. I'd rub the old lamp—or in God's case, I'd pray—and the genie would pop out and grant me three wishes. But if I wasn't careful (or specific) with my ask, I could end up getting *exactly* what I asked for. We've seen these kinds of cringeworthy scenes play out a million times in the movies, right?

I had to face the truth: my thinking was in error if I believed that praying for patience would result in God sending trials my way.

Those who believe in the equation *prayer + trials = patience* also wrongly embrace the notion that if they don't pray for patience, they somehow will avoid having trials and tests in their lives. So I will give credit where credit is due and thank this desert season for helping me at least dig out bad theology. But I couldn't help digressing a bit. I mean, only a nut would wish themselves into a fiery furnace!

When the dry desert air smothered me to the point that I couldn't take it anymore, I found myself asking my pastor a question: "How do we feel close to God when we are not in a trial?"

His response was this: "If I'm not in the fire myself, I get into someone else's fire."

No doubt you've heard that derogatory saying, "Those who can't 'do,' teach." Well, I have a confession to make. Even though I'm writing these words, telling you what *you* need to do, I haven't been so good about rolling up my sleeves and crawling into the furnace myself.

In fact, last summer I absolutely blew it.

My friend Michele was in one of those terrible "life fires" my pastor was talking about. Her very sweet, humble mother—someone who was graceful and kind to everyone she ever met—did the unthinkable: she took her own life.

Michele was devastated.

In fact, the pain is still so raw for Michele and her family, I'm struggling to share her story. But here is what encourages me: my friend is emerging from the ashes as one of the bravest people I know. Michele has used this horrible experience to speak openly about mental health issues, and she often reaches out to others who have endured this kind of loss.

Amazingly, she doesn't run from her grief, and she uses every opportunity to witness for Jesus. "Someday," Michele says, "everything we've lost will be redeemed in full."

I'm so proud of her, and I bet her mom is too.

The thing I'm not proud of is *my* reaction to Michele's loss. When I first heard the news, I froze. I wasn't even brave enough to go to her mom's funeral service. Sure, I sent

> "Someday," Michele says, "everything we've lost will be redeemed in full."

the family the usual "I am so sorry" type sympathies. And I truly do care. I wept openly for Michele and her family, and I still do when I read her posts on Facebook. She misses her mom, and she has so many unanswered questions inside.

Here's what bothers me most about my reaction when someone is in need: there are times when I run and hide behind a facade of busyness when there are people out there standing in an inferno. Why? Sometimes it feels too much for me. (Can you relate?) Yet because I make it about me, there's little wonder I find myself in a desert.

Again, it isn't about me. It is about others and the stuff that's consuming them.

Some people are especially blessed with the gift of pastoring hurting people. This does not come naturally to me, and I usually tell myself that I'm not equipped or strong enough to help support the sadness of others. Yet I think most of us are much abler than we realize to comfort grieving people. God's Spirit not only gives us the power to deal with our own burdens; He equips us to share the load and help carry the burdens of others.

Eventually I made a conscious effort to get out of the desert and get into the fire with someone else. How about you? I know God never left me, but He feels alive in me again. My prayer life is better, and I am learning so much.

As we touch those who hurt, it's okay to hurt with them. Sometimes it's inconvenient, yet we need to reach out anyway. Sometimes it's uncomfortable, yet we need to comfort them anyway. It doesn't matter if we don't know what to say. We need to show up anyway.

We need to pray with them and share some wise words from my friend Michele: "Someday everything we've lost will be redeemed in full."

Lord Jesus, I know that hurting people aren't hard to find. They're the ones on fire. Please give me the courage to jump into the fire with them. And give others the courage to jump into the fire with me when I hurt. Amen.

# CHAPTER 29

# THE SPIRITUAL GIFT OF A BARTENDER'S FACE

*As God's chosen ones, holy and beloved, clothe yourselves*
*with compassion, kindness, humility, meekness, and*
*patience. Bear with one another and, if anyone has a*
*complaint against another, forgive each other; just as*
*the Lord has forgiven you, so you also must forgive.*
*Above all, clothe yourselves with love, which binds*
*everything together in perfect harmony. And let the*
*peace of Christ rule in your hearts, to which indeed*
*you were called in the one body. And be thankful.*
COLOSSIANS 3:12–15 NRSV

I've always been that person who people confided in. Even when I was young, adults would tell me things that were none of my beeswax. I didn't try to get them to tell me things. Most of the time, I really didn't want to know some of the things they would share. I would think, *Look,*

*lady, I'm sorry that you're in crisis mode right now, but I'm just trying to get through puberty here!* All types of people have told me their secrets. I've heard about people's meth problems, affairs, and even personally sensitive things like abuse they had endured in their past.

As a young adult, I was so puzzled by these occurrences I actually asked a friend of mine, "What is it about me that makes people want to tell me their problems?" My friend said, "You have a bartender's face."

A bartender's face? Am I some old guy with a wrinkled shirt and five o'clock shadow? We've all seen them in the movies. The matter-of-fact bartender quietly wiping the bar top while someone spills his or her problems between handfuls of mixed nuts. No matter the story, the bartender just keeps drying the glasses and wiping the bar with a steady expression on his face. In the movies, the person at the bar usually carries on the one-sided conversation until they come to their own moment of clarity.

I'm not an old, crusty bartender. But I obviously have the ability to listen to people's problems without having a strong reaction. Early on in my Christian life, I was sure that my gift was apologetics (the study of the defense of Christianity). I studied the Word, researched the biblical account, and was ready to defend the faith. This came from years of previously trying to discount Christianity. I knew the arguments against Jesus because I had had the same questions for years. So once I came into a relationship with God, I was sure that I was supposed to use this information to convince others of the truth. But instead I realized I have the gift of having a bartender's face.

This was not the spiritual gift I wanted. But it was a skill I had been perfecting all my life. To this day, people with problems still

> I'm not an old, crusty bartender. But I obviously have the ability to listen to people's problems without having a strong reaction.

gravitate toward me and share their life stories. My demeanor has not changed either. I sit with a deadpan expression, listening to their private struggles. That's all a bartender's face is—listening. Taking the time to look someone in the eye while they share their pain, their past, and their desperate need for a Savior helps folks feel important and cared for. It is a skill that's hard to find these days. Showing God's love to someone in need is at the heart of His mission in this world. In this way, I get to be an embodiment of God's love.

Jesus is our example. He was a great listener to those who were searching for redemption and salvation. He sat and listened to the Samaritan woman at the well. He spoke with the blind beggars on the street. Scripture reveals that He was able to tune people in. We are called to the same mission of listening and caring for those in our everyday lives. We may not always have the perfect words to speak. We may not know the solution to a person's problem. But we do know that God loves them and that they are very important in His eyes. This is what we can all bring to the world.

Even if you are not gifted with a bartender's face, you can always focus on taking the time to listen. Ask questions to help others talk out their feelings and questions. Show genuine concern as you pay attention to their worries. And if the Holy Spirit opens the door, be ready to share how much God cares for them during their time of need.

Lord, clothe me with compassion, kindness, humility, meekness, and patience. Help me bear with others, sharing hope and joy in You. Amen.

CHAPTER 30

# JUICY GRACE

*About midnight Paul and Silas were praying and singing*
*hymns to God, and the other prisoners were listening to*
*them. Suddenly there was such a violent earthquake that*
*the foundations of the prison were shaken. At once all the*
*prison doors flew open, and everyone's chains came loose.*
ACTS 16:25–26

Since my husband is a touring comedian, and I often go with him, I am always needing to find a hairdresser in the cities we visit—which means I always have a revolving door of hairdressers to witness to. And depending on what city I find myself in, I usually seek out the first available stylist I can find. Just like bartenders, hairdressers get the life story of every soul who walks through their doors. My story is one of them.

Last winter, while on a trip to Las Vegas, I made an appointment to get my road-weary hair washed and blown out. But then I had second thoughts the night before. Even though I like the end result after a little pampering, it's not how I spend my time back home on the farm. I'm a country girl with better things to do! Just as I picked up my phone to cancel, I sensed the Lord nudging me to stick with my plans. *Is this really from God?* I wondered. *Is He giving me an opportunity to share my faith?*

"Okay, Lord," I prayed. "I'll stop being so lazy, and I'll go."

The next day as I climbed into the stylist's chair, I was greeted by a young hairdresser named Kelly. As she shook my hand, I noticed right away that both her arms were covered in full-sleeve tattoos. *Yes!* I thought to myself.

I always get excited by the sight of a tattoo on a stranger because it instantly opens a door to a conversation. And as I bring attention to a person's body art, it usually sets them at ease, showing that I'm not uptight or judgmental about their style preferences.

> I always get excited by the sight of a tattoo on a stranger because it instantly opens a door to a conversation.

Since Jesus is silent on the topic of getting ink, I believe that tattoos fall under the category of a "gray area" of faith. Believers should follow their own convictions while respecting the convictions of others. I say this because I've met other Christians who have strong opinions about tattoos. If that describes you, I encourage you to start a conversation. Learn why another person is inked. It's often very personal, and if it is important to them, it should be important to you.

I usually start with small talk, breaking the ice with the person I just met. And then I start a conversation that goes something like this: "I can't help but notice your tattoos. Tell me about what they mean to you. I always love to hear about a person's artwork."

Most of the time, the people I talk with feel as if it's easier just to cover up, so they're usually excited to tell the story behind their tattoos.

As I got to know Kelly, I learned that she was battling an addiction to alcohol, but that she'd been sober for more than six months.

"It's the hardest thing I've ever had to deal with," Kelly said as she brushed my hair. "But it feels better to be sober, so I'm not giving up. And where I live is really helping me. I'm renting a small place on a horse ranch. I love horses. They seem to get my mind off my problems."

Suddenly, my ears perked up. God just kicked open the "conversation door" with a huge opportunity. "Did you just say 'horses'?" I blurted. "I

> "I love horses. They seem to get my mind off my problems."

own a herd of them in Nebraska, and I live on a horse ranch too! Actually, it's a farm."

I shared my love of horses and how I'd written a book about them. "It's called *Unbridled Faith*," I explained. "In it, I talk about my faith—the spiritual lessons that have brought me closer to God through horses."

Kelly's brush strokes slowed a bit, and her eyes became moist. "That's just what I need," she said, "what I've been looking for. I need God."

As tears rolled down her cheeks, she told me she was looking for meaning in life. "One day I just started talking to God," Kelly added. "I asked if there was more."

I told her about Jesus and how much He loves her right where she is—just as she is. By the end of my appointment, as I was heading out the door, I gave her one of my books. (Yep—I came prepared!) We even agreed to stay in touch.

Today—many, many months later—Kelly is still sober. Although she hasn't committed her life to Christ yet, God is still working on her. And He's a good Father who will never, ever abandon her.

Has God ever kicked open the "conversation door" for you? I bet He has. Think about all the times you were where you were because God put you there. Think about the divine appointments He has orchestrated in your life.

Every time we open our mouths and declare the good news, someone could be listening. Nothing can shackle the power of the gospel! And I noticed as I was talking to Kelly, the whole salon had an ear tipped in my direction. A fellow patron even said, "That's right!" when I got to the juicy parts about Jesus. That's good gossip that we need to spread. Just like the apostle Paul, we can find an audience wherever we go. Other prisoners and even a jailer became the unsuspecting target of Paul's gospel.

Divine appointments may not even be about the person you are going to see. You may be there to witness to another person in the room who just might need to overhear this nugget: "Jesus loves you enough to die for you!"

Wowza! That's juicy grace that needs to be shared.

.................................................................................................

Lord, thank You for the divine appointments You have put in my life. Help me always be ready to share my faith in You. Help me never to miss an opportunity. Amen.

CHAPTER 31

# MY TRUTH TIME BOMB

*To the Jews who had believed him, Jesus said, "If you hold*
*to my teaching, you are really my disciples. Then you*
*will know the truth, and the truth will set you free."*
JOHN 8:31–32

One of the most mind-blowing acts of friendship in my life came from my neighbors Bart and Brenda. I have said to them that Jesus commands us to love our neighbors as ourselves, but with neighbors like them it's not really that difficult of an ask. I know the word *neighbor* extends to everyone in the world, but it's just a fun way to tell my neighbors how much I love and appreciate them.

About three years ago, one of my horses, Sven (a.k.a. Fat Benny), came down with strangles. This condition is like equine strep throat, only way more complicated, and it can be deadly. To this day I have no idea how Sven contracted it, but he did. Sven was so sick he'd stopped pooping. So there I was one night at about 10:00 p.m., praying my horse would poop. Horses that can't poop will die, period. So once I came to the conclusion that my prayers weren't going to manifest themselves into the steaming pile I was hoping for, I decided that Sven should be taken to the K-State Veterinary Health Center in Manhattan, Kansas. (It's on the campus of Kansas State University.)

So there I was one night at about 10:00 p.m., praying my horse would poop.

Both my kids were small at the time, and my husband was out of town working, but my neighbors graciously offered to take Sven on the three-plus-hour drive to the K-State facility. With tears in my eyes, I hugged my equine friend for possibly the last time and then prayed, holding hands together with my neighbors in a dirty horse arena. As red taillights left out the gate toward Kansas, I praised God that I was not alone and that I had good friends who gave up their time that night because they loved me. I don't think Bart and Brenda even made it back to Nebraska until 4:00 a.m., and they both had to work later that morning.

Time is one of the hardest things to give to someone. I think we always think about sacrificing money or even our lives, but we never really think about how important time is and why we don't want to give it up.

I was in a Bible study once, and my friend Carolyn told us about her neighbor who had broken her leg. She then told us that she (Carolyn) was not being obedient to the Lord's prompting. As a newer believer at the time, I asked her what she meant by that. Carolyn said, "When the Lord prompted me to go over to her house and ask her if she needed help with anything, I didn't go. It took me two days to go over there and offer my help. I ended up helping her get her mail, which was easy, so I am not sure why it took me so long to go to her." When Carolyn told me that, it really opened my eyes up to the fact that I, too, was extremely stingy with my time. For me it's not just getting the mail, but the fear that whatever I volunteer to do may end up being a full-blown commitment to something.

God is the only one not racing the clock, because He *is* the clock. He's never early or late; He can stop a day if He wants or make a day last a thousand years or more. He also will not tell us when He is going to come back. So there is my dilemma; it could be today, tomorrow, or six hundred years from now. I guess what I am trying to say is I live my life like it's probably going to be more like the six hundred years from now. I don't feel like I'm under the gun, and I don't have to give people more of my time than is absolutely necessary. It's why I'm not at the homeless shelter slopping potatoes. It's not that I lack compassion. I just don't want to give up my time. Do you see what kind of rat I'm exposing here? As much as I weep for the lost, if I'm not careful, my sin nature would rather spend time vegging on the couch watching *Dateline* than taking the time to fill the needs of others.

That makes me think about the wise men from the East who brought baby Jesus the three symbolic gifts of gold, frankincense, and myrrh. Jesus was over a year old before they made it to the house where He was. The gifts were great and all, but what

> God is the only one not racing the clock, because He *is* the clock.

about the time it took for them to get there? I say I love Jesus, but then, well, you know . . . something good may be on TV.

I've been working hard lately to make lost souls a priority in the present. Like a Jesus-is-coming-back-today priority. Or to put it another way,

I think a lot about my "truth time bomb" and the importance of avoiding time-wasters. I need to focus on the right stuff—loving God, loving others, doing kingdom work—before I'm out of time. This does not come naturally to me like it does to Bart and Brenda, but thankfully I serve an awesome God who gently exposes the parts of myself that I need to improve on. He's making me a better witness because He truly knows that time is of the essence.

And by the way, Sven pulled through and made it safely back to Nebraska. I can't stop thanking my friends Bart and Brenda!

Lord, help me steer clear of distractions in life and learn to focus on what's important to You. Amen.

CHAPTER 32

# MESSES TO MESSAGES

*[The jailer] brought [Paul and Silas] out and said, "Sirs,*
*what must I do to be saved?" And they said, "Believe in the*
*Lord Jesus, and you will be saved, you and your household."*
*And they spoke the word of the Lord to him and to all who*
*were in his house. And he took them the same hour of the*
*night and washed their wounds; and he was baptized at*
*once, he and all his family. Then he brought them up into*
*his house and set food before them. And he rejoiced along*
*with his entire household that he had believed in God.*

ACTS 16:30–34 ESV

It's not always horses that have taken me on the wildest rides in my life—and believe me, I have eaten dirt plenty of times. To be honest, the hardest hits have come from horse people I thought I could trust but who turned out to be con artists in disguise.

I always say that horse people are never lukewarm. They are usually salt-of-the-earth-type folk or they are intensely toxic. Why are they so polarized? I have no idea, but I have experienced my fair share of both. These days I am lucky to be surrounded by only the salt-of-the-earth horse owners, due mostly to the fact that (for a moment) I am taking a break from buying and showing horses.

I had purchased a horse from a woman on the East Coast a few years back. By the time the transport truck showed up, an unbroken horse stepped off that I suspected was from a sale barn and not her supposed show barn. This unscrupulous woman had sent me a different horse than the one I purchased. The animal I bought was supposed to be twelve years old and "husband safe." But after an inspection by our vet, because this poor horse also came to us covered in rain rot, he concluded that this animal was probably only about three years old. And by the way, it almost killed my husband. Imagine that scene, Dan on the back of this beast that was bucking like a rodeo bronc. Incredibly, Dan rode it out (and he wanted me to let you know that).

When I called the woman and suggested with certainty that she had sent me the wrong horse, she faked a bad phone connection and then would not pick up when I tried calling back.

> This unscrupulous woman had sent me a different horse than the one I purchased.

Why is it when we get taken advantage of or swindled like that, we are the ones left feeling as if we have done something wrong? I was so embarrassed, and I felt so stupid.

After much prayer, I decided God was giving me an amazing opportunity to witness to this lost soul and that I needed to respond to this circumstance with an action that she would never expect. Instead of involving an attorney and serving her with the papers she truly deserved, I decided to serve her with a Bible instead. In its pages I had handwritten a note that included the gospel. I let her know that I had forgiven her, and I went on to say that if she didn't want the Bible, to at least put it in a drawer for a day when she may want some hope.

I'd like to think that I offered her something Christlike enough that it made an impact on her the moment she received it. But also it'd be safe to say that some people really don't want to hear what we have to say. If she hasn't read it yet, I pray that she has at least put it away until the day her heart is prepared enough to hear what its pages have to say.

Because God turns messes into messages, this story does go on to have a happy ending here in Nebraska. We gave that misrepresented horse to our neighbor Brenda, along with some training. Lucas has grown to become Brenda's number one trail horse. Our sale barn mishap has been redeemed.

It also takes a lot more than our persuasive powers to convince others that Jesus is the Savior.

At the end of the day, a true seeker really wants to know the truth, and no amount of arguing, trickery, or manipulation is going to make their heart beat for Jesus. I know from my own experience that I had to get to a point where I just wanted to know the truth.

Sure, my wallet took a hit that day on a bad horse deal. But I'd rather see heaven gain a soul than worry about my hurt pride. For people to be changed by Christ, they must first come in contact with Him, so we have to live tactfully and not get discouraged even when others embarrass us or make us feel stupid.

> I'd rather see heaven gain a soul than worry about my hurt pride.

Let Scripture remind us about the Philippian jailer who in the book of Acts didn't have a change of heart after hearing a lecture, but rather after hearing just one sentence: "Believe in the Lord Jesus, and you will be saved, you and your household."

When the heart is prepared, the odds are good that you won't need that much convincing to lead another to the Savior. Keep it clear and most of all sincere. When God swings open a door of opportunity, we just have to be ready to enter.

...................................................................................

Lord, help me always be available and willing to lead someone to You—even those who mistreat me. Amen.

# CHAPTER 33

# SALT YOUR CONVERSATIONS

*"You are like salt for everyone on earth. But if salt no longer tastes like salt, how can it make food salty? All it is good for is to be thrown out and walked on."*
MATTHEW 5:13 CEV

I was amazed to learn that horses spend more than 14.5 hours per day grazing! Then I started laughing because I thought, *Well, that's just another way I can relate to my horses.*

Right now the fall leaves are changing, and the comfort foods are trying to seduce me. Since I'm from Wisconsin, the temptation of a cheddar-covered casserole is winning. I even stopped buying fall-scented candles because they made me want to end every meal with a slice of pumpkin pie. I really have to watch myself this time of year. I think this applies to most people, and that's why by January we are all pondering the idea of purchasing gym equipment.

As for my plump ponies, I have to help them watch their weight too. Chubby horses can have all kinds of health issues, and some of these conditions can even become life-threatening. So my remedy has been to use a slow-feeding hay net. It's a net made of strong nylon that I toss over a round bale of hay. It is designed with small holes that my horses can eat through. A slow-feeding hay net slows the rate of forage intake and increases the amount of time it takes horses to eat a hay meal.[1] It makes me wonder if they make hay nets for people!

Recently I started attending a Pilates class in order to regain some of my core strength. It's also a terrific way to get out of the house so I can witness for Christ. God doesn't command the lost to go to church, but He does command us to go out to the lost. So . . . I go to Pilates. It's a win-win.

I haven't found any lost souls there yet, though. As it turns out, most everyone I have met in class is already a believer. But this adventure has been very encouraging to my faith and to theirs. It's an hour of iron sharpening iron, and as we get stronger physically, we grow spiritually as well.

Lots of people ask me how to share their faith because it's such an awkward thing to bring up the topic of Jesus. But I can turn that question around on them and ask, "I never told you I was a follower of Jesus, so how did you know?" It is possible to have fruitful interactions with people so nonchalantly that people don't even realize I am laying the groundwork for witnessing. I call it salting the conversation. It's basically putting a few grains of spiritual "salt" into your conversations so people know you are a believer. For example, you can say something like this: "Last Sunday my pastor shared a story about the human side of Jesus that I never knew. Here's what he said. . . ." Salting your words and sharing insights about Christ casually and naturally are great ways to share your faith.

It is possible to have fruitful interactions with people so nonchalantly that people don't even realize I am laying the groundwork for witnessing.

You will be amazed at how easy it is, and in the same way that salt enhances the flavor of the food it seasons, followers of Christ stand out as those who "enhance" the flavor of life in this world.[2]

Just as I set my horses up with slow-feeding hay nets, salting our conversations and offering others a slow and steady amount of Christ are better than dumping the overwhelming idea of a complete lifestyle change on their plates.

More salt in conversations and less on French fries. It's a win-win.

. . . . . . . . . . . . . . . . . . . . . . . . . . . . . . . . . . . . . . . . . . . . . . . . . . . . . . . . . . . . . . . . . . . . . . . . . . .

Lord, help me be salt and light. Please open opportunities to share my faith and give me the right words to share at the right moment—words seasoned with salt. Amen.

# CHAPTER 34

# GO, AND STAY OUT OF THE GARBAGE

*Then those who heard it, being convicted by their conscience,
went out one by one, beginning with the oldest even to the
last. And Jesus was left alone, and the woman standing in
the midst. When Jesus had raised Himself up and saw no
one but the woman, He said to her, "Woman, where are
those accusers of yours? Has no one condemned you?"
She said, "No one, Lord."
And Jesus said to her, "Neither do I
condemn you; go and sin no more."*
JOHN 8:9–11 NKJV

My first dog was a basset hound named Wilma. The second I laid eyes on her, I had my own *Casablanca* moment: "Wilma, I think this is the beginning of a beautiful friendship."

The year was 1992, and I worked at a radio station in La Crosse,

Wisconsin. While doing a remote broadcast from the Valley View Mall, I made the fateful mistake of letting curiosity get the best of me. During a break I slipped into a nearby pet store. I quickly made my way past the wall-to-wall aquariums and stinky bird cages and sweet-talked a clerk into letting me snuggle with the puppies.

That's when it happened.

Right there before my eyes was the longest dog I'd ever seen. She was white with black and brown polka dots, long brown ears that grazed the floor, and four meaty three-inch legs. She was a stunner! And so began a love story between a single girl and a floppy-eared dog that would span over fourteen years.

As I chased my young-adult dreams, she was right there with me: her nose stuck out the window, her ears flopping in the wind, riding along in the back seat of my Pontiac Grand Am. We were inseparable—even to the point of Wilma developing separation anxiety. My heading off to work in the morning gradually became a problem for my furry friend. She'd get lonely and would chew up stuff during the day, including the windowsills in my apartment. I tried putting her in a kennel. Bad idea. When I returned home in the afternoon to check on her, she had poop all over herself—on the cage, outside the cage, everywhere. Yuck!

Wilma ended up getting us both evicted, yet I refused to give up on her. I loved her too much to let her go. So I tried harder to fix the problem: medication, training, advice from well-meaning friends, daily doggie belly rubs with tender tickles behind the ears. (She loved those!) And then it hit me: *she's lonely.*

I finally got another dog to be Wilma's companion. Problem solved.

> Right there before my eyes was the longest dog I'd ever seen.

Wilma and I had been through thick and thin together. We shared an unbreakable bond—the kind that only trials and time can create. She was with me when I moved off the family farm and right there with me as I hopped from city to city, pursuing my radio career. She was there when I married Dan and there when I gave birth to my kids. But life moves on.

Eventually Wilma passed away from cancer at almost fifteen years of age. To this day, I tear up when I think about her. I miss her so much, especially that half-bark, half-howling sound that only hound dogs make. She lived the good life, and I was definitely her servant! She was the most selfish dog I ever loved.

She was the most selfish dog I ever loved.

I wonder why we go happily into dog ownership, knowing they will probably chew up our furniture, pee on the carpet, get in the garbage, or roll in dead frog. (My list could take up this whole page!) Yet we expect more from people whose sin nature abounds.

In John 8, we learn about a woman who had been caught in the act of adultery. When the woman's accusers brought her before Jesus, expecting Him to pronounce judgment, He told them that the one who was without sin should throw the first stone. One by one, the condemning crowd left. Then Jesus told the woman, "Neither do I condemn you; go and sin no more."

Of all those men, Jesus was the only one without sin—which means He was the only one who had a right to condemn, yet He didn't. It took me a while to understand the significance of the word order of "*Go and sin no more.*" Do you see it too? In Christ, pardon is given first; but with religion, the order is reversed.

I have gotten that wrong. I have been religious. I know I have almost set back a new believer because I was so concerned about their continued sin. Thankfully, the Holy Spirit prompted me to apologize to them and—thankfully—they forgave me. I am not without sin, and it is not my right to condemn anyone.

As Jesus commanded in John 8:9–11, we must strive to "go and sin no more." I recognize that, but while we are in the flesh, we are going to make a mess on the carpet sometimes.

> I am not without sin, and it is not my right to condemn anyone.

There is a difference between continuing to sin and continuing to live in sin. None of us will reach sinless perfection in this life, but we are the redeemed who are being sanctified (made holy) day by day, sinning less and hating it more each time we fail. Yes, we may still mess up and sin from time to time, but we'll probably discover it happening less frequently as we grow in our faith. God tends to create bonds with His children with trials and time. I have to be careful not to damage the gospel message for someone by putting expectations on a new believer. I can't treat a new believer the same way I'd treat a mature Christ-follower.

As believers, we need to witness to the people in this world the way we love our dogs: "Yes, Fido, you ate deer poop in the park, but I love you too much to just walk away."

Lord, keep me from turning into the person who is so focused on someone else's sin that I miss the true spirit of the one command: "Love your neighbor as yourself." Amen.

# CHAPTER 35

# FRIEND OF SINNERS

*"John came neither eating nor drinking, and they*
*say, 'He has a demon'; the Son of Man came eating*
*and drinking, and they say, 'Look, a glutton and a*
*drunkard, a friend of tax collectors and sinners!'*
*Yet wisdom is vindicated by her deeds."*
MATTHEW 11:18–19 NRSV

If you're thinking about adopting a rescue dog, I hope you'll do it. Not only will she nuzzle her way into your heart with daily, unspoken appreciation—that wagging tail and puppy-dog expression say it all—she'll also teach you a lot about second chances.

Abby Doobins is a rescue dog that has been with us just a little over a year now. While she has the same body shape as a black lab, her legs are only about eight inches long . . . so there's not a whole lot of clearance between her undercarriage and the ground! A recent DNA test revealed that she is 62.8 percent golden retriever, with a dollop of chihuahua and a pinch of miniature schnauzer. After that the Lord just started throwing spare dog parts into the recipe. Abby is definitely one of a kind, and we love *mostly* everything about her. Let me emphasize the word *mostly*. We love all things Abby except for her propensity to roll in all things stinky. In the last two days I've had to give her portly body three separate baths.

In spite of her fascination with filth, we wouldn't change a thing about her.

We love all things Abby except for her propensity to roll in all things stinky.

One night as my husband was watching TV, Abby hopped onto his lap, curled up, and rested her chin on his knee—as if to say, "I'm happy, and I'm safe, and I wouldn't want to be anywhere else in the world but right here with my favorite person."

An expression of pure joy washed over Dan's face. "You know," he said, "I really think God brought this dog to me."

It's true. Abby will never gain a trophy for her pedigree, but what she lacks in breeding, she makes up for in authenticity and heart.

We read in the Bible that Jesus was accused of being a "friend of sinners." They called Him that because it was true.[1] Jesus Himself said that He didn't come for the spiritually healthy, but for the sick.[2] "It is not the healthy who need a doctor, but the sick. I have not come to call the righteous, but sinners to repentance" (Luke 5:31–32).

Jesus made friends with everyday, ordinary people—many with low pedigrees by society's standards, and some who were accused of "rolling in filth." Yet the folks Jesus associated with had authenticity and heart, and whether or not they were crude or socially unacceptable, He shared meals, smiles, and stories with them. Just imagine the crude language He must've heard as He broke bread with them. Still, Jesus wasn't repulsed. He just reclined and enjoyed a moment with them.

I get so frustrated as I try to distinguish between what is and isn't "allowable" to God based on the standards set by other Christians. It seems a few times a year when I open up my social media account, there is at least one Christian group that is calling for other Christians to boycott something they feel is too "worldly." Movies, businesses, video games, and sometimes even people will make their list of immoral things. Is this the difference between people who live by faith in religion and faith in Christ Jesus?

> Jesus made friends with everyday, ordinary people—many with low pedigrees by society's standards, and some who were accused of "rolling in filth."

About a month ago, I checked my Instagram account and noticed that one of my friends had posted a video of himself drunk and getting lap dances from several women. It was cringeworthy by my Christian standard, but what I really found myself doing was expecting someone who is not a follower of Jesus to act like they followed Him. Dare I say I found myself becoming religious. Even worse, I'd forgotten how far I've come.

I'm not sure it's even possible to avoid contact with immoral people or businesses that support ungodly practices, because to do so, we would have to leave the world. If I continue to set unreachable goals for the world to follow, I run the risk of leading unbelievers toward the idea that everything I say I follow is a bunch of horse hockey—especially because there is no way I would be able to live up to my own standard. But we also have to love someone enough to tell them the truth about their sin. This is an act of compassion, as long as it is done with humility and true love.

We share our faith more effectively as we learn to strike a balance between the two. In other words, we can keep our Christian membership card and still be friends with sinners.

Let's be clear, Jesus does *not* condone sin. He also didn't allow others who were rolling in all things stinky to influence Him. So if we're going to be like Jesus in the world, we need to quit viewing unbelievers as if they are our enemies. We need to stand strong enough in our own convictions to prevent worldly ideas from rubbing off on us. Just as when I carry Abby to the washroom, I need to be careful that whatever she's been rolling in doesn't rub off on me.

We shouldn't let cultural norms dictate to whom we evangelize, and we need to learn to ignore the opinions of those who are religious. The sick need a physician. Being a friend of sinners means not always approving of everything your friends do, yet loving them anyway—even as they are rolling in it.

Lord, show me how to be a friend of sinners. Help me love those who are different from me, even those who are "rolling in filth." Protect me from that filth, and show me how to love, share a moment, and lead others to Your eternal love. Amen.

# CHAPTER 36

# THE STREET-CORNER COATRACK

*Religion that God our Father accepts as pure and faultless*
*is this: to look after orphans and widows in their distress*
*and to keep oneself from being polluted by the world.*

JAMES 1:27

I see pain and brokenness all around me. In my own small town—a hardworking Nebraska farm community—children and homeless families go hungry. Some huddle near busy intersections, clutching tattered signs: "NEED FOOD." "UNEMPLOYED VET." "HELP MY FAMILY."

And when I head into the city, it feels even worse.

Actually, everywhere I travel in this great country of ours—from Los Angeles to Baltimore—I see people in need. There are places in Chicago and St. Louis where whole neighborhoods are made up of crumbling homes and dilapidated churches. In Detroit and New York City there are streets that look more like abandoned war zones than habitable communities. Windows are smashed out, roofs are caving in, and graffiti covers everything.

Here's something else I've learned: if we slow down and take a closer look at these places—instead of just zooming past them—we'll see families who are trying to make sense of it all. Peeking out of some of those shattered windows are men, women, and children who are barely holding on. It breaks my heart, and I'm sure it breaks yours too.

All throughout the Bible, God calls us to show compassion to the poor and the needy. Jesus said that they would always be with us (Matthew 26:11; Mark 14:7), but He also said that those who show mercy to the poor, the sick, and the needy are in effect ministering to Him personally and will be rewarded.

Then the King will say to those on his right, "Come, you who are blessed by my Father, inherit the kingdom prepared for you from the foundation of the world. For I was hungry and you gave me food, I was thirsty and you gave me drink, I was a stranger and you welcomed me, I was naked and you clothed me, I was sick and you visited me, I was in prison and you came to me." Then the righteous will answer him, saying, "Lord, when did we see you hungry and feed you, or thirsty and give you drink? And when did we see you a stranger and welcome you, or naked and clothe you? And when did we see you sick or in prison and visit you?" And the King will answer them, "Truly, I say to you, as you did it to one of the least of these my brothers, you did it to me." (Matthew 25:34–40 ESV)

Still, I can't help feeling overwhelmed by all the needs around me, and I often feel as if my hands are tied. I mean, how can a country girl in Nebraska help a hungry kid in St. Louis . . . or Chicago or New York City?

Recently a friend was sharing a similar frustration. He and his wife live just outside of St. Louis, and they often feel overwhelmed by all the needs in their city. But one winter evening, as they were driving home after a day spent sightseeing around the Arch, they encountered something on the side of the road that made them pull over and take notice.

Just outside a pub in an urban neighborhood they spotted a long rack filled with coats of every color and size. Above the rack was a handwritten sign that read, "Stay warm! Please take a jacket . . . or leave one for someone else!"

The bartenders had found a simple way to clothe the needy and touch their community, and that inspired my friends. They

Above the rack was a handwritten sign that read, "Stay warm! Please take a jacket . . . or leave one for someone else!"

immediately started brainstorming all kinds of ways they could minister in their neighborhood. "It was a perfect reminder for God's people," the husband told me. "It's time to get off our pews and go into the world."

We cannot be indifferent toward those in need, because the Lord's challenge to take care of the poor is woven throughout Scripture. And we don't have to feel clueless about what to do. There are lots of simple ways we can go in to the broken, painful places all around us and minister in God's name.

A country girl can take a sack of groceries to a neighbor in need. A city couple can bring a trunkload of jackets to a street-corner coatrack. "Truly, I say to you, as you did it to one of the least of these my brothers, you did it to me."

Lord, help me slow down and see those peering out of shattered windows in broken communities. I, too, want to feed the hungry and clothe the needy in Your name. I want to bring hope and healing to a hurting world. Amen.

CHAPTER 37

# SERVING IN THE SHADOWS

*"You are the light of the world. A city set on a hill*
*cannot be hidden. Nor do people light a lamp and put*
*it under a basket, but on a stand, and it gives light to*
*all in the house. In the same way, let your light shine*
*before others, so that they may see your good works*
*and give glory to your Father who is in heaven."*
MATTHEW 5:14–16 ESV

Sometimes I get so angry with what I read online, I feel like taking down my main social media account. People on the Internet are representing some devilishly dark corners through their opinions and lifestyles.

But just when I'm ready to pull the plug, Jesus reminds me that we need to step out of our Christian bubbles and serve in the shadows.

I admit, I love dwelling in the comfortable regions of my life—those places where the good news is always well received and the idea of service happens within the body of my church. Although service within the

church body is expected—and the church always has a need—Scripture calls us to go into the world and into the lives of people who are most in need of God's light. Jesus' idea of service is not being comfortable in a building, but instead going into areas where people are encased in spiritual darkness.

It was not by chance that Jesus started His public ministry in the city of Capernaum, which was also known as "the land of the shadow of death" (Matthew 4:16). Jesus always made sure to put Himself around the people who were most in need of His healing and guidance. Since the Capernaum inhabitants were wading in spiritual yuck, the Great Physician shined His light into this region's darkest corners by performing many miracles there.

> Jesus' idea of service is not being comfortable in a building, but instead going into areas where people are encased in spiritual darkness.

Jesus wants to perform miracles through us. He wants us to love people beyond what this world deems reasonable. It's what Jesus commands us to do, and maybe He knows that for some of us, like myself, trying to love hard hearts *is* a miracle.

I recently asked myself if I had a Capernaum in my life. I discovered that social media is that place for me. That's when the Holy Spirit told me to stay in Capernaum a little while longer. Social media is one of the places the gospel is needed most and where good news can easily be spread. Just when I want to quit, I get a perfectly timed message from someone that puts my mission back on track. I come into contact daily with people who are craving the light on social media. It was sad to think I was "unfriending" these same people because their cultural views didn't always fall in line with mine.

I come into contact daily with people who are craving the light on social media.

When it seems like a waste of time to continue evangelizing unbelievers and hardened hearts, that's when I do my best to pray hard for them. Why would I even think Jesus' message could penetrate through all that treachery? Here's my answer: it's because Jesus prayed for His enemies on the cross, and a hardened criminal found forgiveness, and a Roman centurion acknowledged Jesus as the Son of God. (See Luke 23:26–49.)

I admit that sometimes it feels next to impossible to extend kindness toward the hard people God places in my life. But I try to remember two things: I'm not in Capernaum to win an argument, but a soul. And I'm not condoning sin by being kind. So I am choosing to love the way Jesus teaches me to love. As I share His love with those who don't yet know Him, I am actually shining His eternal light into the dark corners of someone's life.

So ask yourself, "Where is the Capernaum in my life?" And then go there and have meaningful encounters with people who are living hard lives.

Lord, thank You for coming into the darkness of my life. Now let me use Your example of love to shine some light into a darkened world. Amen.

# CHAPTER 38

# TWO STEPS FORWARD, ONE STEP BACK

*He said to me, "My grace is all you need. My power is strongest when you are weak." So I am very happy to brag about how weak I am. Then Christ's power can rest on me. Because of how I suffered for Christ, I'm glad that I am weak. I am glad in hard times. I am glad when people say mean things about me. I am glad when things are difficult. And I am glad when people make me suffer. When I am weak, I am strong.*

2 CORINTHIANS 12:9–10 NIRV

Even though I understand the concept of grace in my head a bit better these days, from time to time I still forget what grace means for me personally.

There are the crabby days, the snap-at-my-husband days, the gossipy days, the yell-at-the-kids (again) days. Days when I beat myself up for being a bad wife, a bad mother, a bad housekeeper, a bad Christian. Days when I can easily convince myself that grace is for others but certainly not for me.

Let me give you an example. A couple of years ago, as the result of a particularly inspiring sermon, Michelle—a Lincoln, Nebraska, housewife who lives across town from me—decided she would aspire to exude grace and peace throughout her day, every day, to whomever crossed her path. Her experiment caught my attention.

The first few hours were a snap. She was patient and cheery, loving and kind. Grace and peace oozed from every pore for four straight hours. The trouble is, a day is long—and frankly, who can exude grace and peace for sixteen consecutive hours?

As it turns out, the vacuum cleaner broke her.

As she pushed the floor brush along the baseboard and beneath the couch, her brand-new vacuum suddenly lost all suction.

Grace and peace oozed from every pore for four straight hours.

She switched the vacuum off, peered into the hose, tapped the attachment on the floor, then switched the vacuum back on. Still nothing. The kids, glimpsing the wild look in her eyes, scurried to their rooms like mice as she heaved attachments and hoses onto the couch, slammed the dirty canister over the garbage can, and stomped back into the living room, muttering furiously under her breath.

"Don't even bother," she fumed to her husband as he patiently detached the hose. "What a complete waste. It's totally broken. My brand-new vacuum is ruined. What a piece of junk! I can't even believe this."

She ranted and raved in full tantrum mode as her husband shined a flashlight into the end of the hose, poked and prodded at it with a pencil, and finally fished out a motley mass of hair, string, brown Christmas tree needles, and an acorn. Then he snapped the canister and hose back into place and switched on the vacuum. It purred sweetly, full suction restored.

Suffice to say, Michelle did not spread grace and peace throughout her home that Saturday. She hadn't even made it through a single day with her good intentions and aspirations intact. She was disappointed and disgusted with herself. And she was embarrassed, seeing as she'd announced her plan to her family in a grand proclamation that very morning, yet she hadn't gotten through five hours before disintegrating into raving lunacy.

I not only identify with and embrace my sister in Christ, I've been there too.

Here's what I learned from her failed grace-and-peace project: good intentions aren't enough. We will fail—over and over again, in spite of our strongest resolve and our best-laid plans. The truth is, we are flawed. We are fallible. We make mistakes. A few of us heave vacuum cleaner parts around the living room. Although Jesus asks us to be perfect, we cannot achieve perfection because we are simply not Him.

Here's what I learned from her failed grace-and-peace project: good intentions aren't enough.

Maybe this is hard for you, this knowledge that you will fail. I know it is for me. I don't like to fail. I set the bar high, and I'm hard on myself when I don't meet it. The key, though, is that God knows that about me, just like He knows all the quirks that make you uniquely you. And He loves us—every part of us—no matter what.

Because of that love, I keep trying, knowing that I will stray, knowing that I will flounder and fail, but also confident that I will survive, thrive, and ultimately, with God's good grace, become a better, humbler, more patient, slightly more Jesus-like person. On some days. And on the days that I fail, well, I'll just start over again.

After all, that's what grace is, right? It's the ultimate do-over, the infinite second chance. God gives us another chance, and another and another. Day in and day out. He works with us and through us. And He doesn't ever give up on us

That's what I believe. That's what I share with those who don't yet know Jesus.[1]

...........................................................................................

Lord, thank You for extending ultimate grace. Thank You for do-overs. Thank You for guiding me through those crabby, snap-at-everyone, gossipy days. Most of all, I'm thankful that You'll never, ever give up on any of us. Amen.

# CHAPTER 39

# DON'T KISS YOUR
# TESTIMONY GOODBYE

*"This is what I say to all who will listen to me: Love
your enemies, and be good to everyone who hates you.
Ask God to bless anyone who curses you, and pray for
everyone who is cruel to you. If someone slaps you on one
cheek, don't stop that person from slapping you on the
other cheek. If someone wants to take your coat, don't
try to keep back your shirt. Give to everyone who asks
and don't ask people to return what they have taken
from you. Treat others just as you want to be treated."*

LUKE 6:27–31 CEV

With the number of horses I own, and my desire to have picturesque pastures free of blemishes, I often hire teenage kids to help me with my "manure management." I love the newbies, but to be honest, they do make me a little nervous because horses are not stupid, and they seem to take great enjoyment from messing with the new help.

For example, my horse Sven's favorite way to accomplish this is to rush the gate when a new person opens it up to pull in the manure cart.

We have security cameras on every angle of our property, so when the new employee gets to the point where they understand the task and it's their time to shine solo, I will watch them on cameras . . . and witness the inevitable. Sure enough, that fat, naughty horse will rush out into the yard, and the help is left standing arms up in distress. They will panic and grab a rope and chase Sven all over the yard until they become exhausted. At that point Sven will stop trotting around and nonchalantly chomp on the grass as the teen just watches—totally exasperated!

At that point, I step in to teach them a great lesson.

We can't always control what horses do, but we can control how we respond to their behavior. In Sven's case, I just walk away and focus on what I need to get done. When the pastures are clean, I grab a rope, walk right up to him, and place it around his neck. Then I calmly lead him back in. It works every time.

> We can't always control
> what horses do, but
> we can control how we
> respond to their behavior.

Here's a news flash: horses can be stinkers, and people are not always lovable either—especially those who drive too slow in the passing lane or those who follow too closely behind us on the highway. This also applies to people who have a cart full of groceries in the line meant for twenty items or less.

We live in a society of in-the-moment, here-and-now people! This kind of attitude isn't right, and these types of annoyances can easily turn us into grace Nazis. "No grace for you!"

The truth is, I'm like most people—often forgetting about grace until I need some myself. So what do I do when I feel stepped on by others or when I simply get fed up with someone's self-centeredness, such as a person who takes up more than one parking space or those who weigh in on something they know nothing about? I simply ask myself, *Do I expect all things in this world to serve me?*

That question is pretty humbling.

If the anger is justified, and sometimes it is, I recommend walking away . . . or not answering that text until everyone has calmed down. We need to take the time to process things and run the issues under the light of God's Word.

What about people who wrongly slander you and use their anger to turn others against you? It's a sure thing that it will happen at some point in life. By no means are we "Christian doormats." But Jesus tells us never to repay an eye for an eye: "But I tell you not to try to get even with a person who has done something to you. When someone slaps your right cheek, turn and let that person slap your other cheek. If someone sues you for your shirt, give up your coat as well" (Matthew 5:39–40 CEV). In other words, take the high road and let God fight your battles.

While we can't control what others say or do, we can control how we respond. I always think to myself, *It's not worth losing my testimony to let this person know they are being rude or inappropriate.*

By no means are we "Christian doormats." But Jesus tells us never to repay an eye for an eye.

People are hard! Keeping our testimony intact is like chasing an ornery horse around the yard. If we ask, Jesus will help us take a deep breath and patiently wait for the horse to stop trotting around. Then we can throw the rope around the horse's neck, take the lead, and shut the gate.

.......................................................................................................

Lord, please give me the strength to love those who aren't very kind to me. Help me treat people the way I want to be treated. Most of all, protect my testimony. Amen.

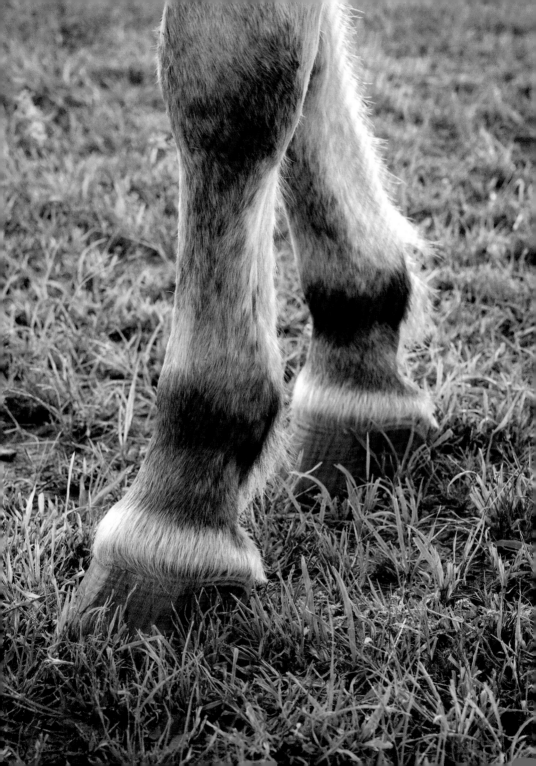

# THE FRIENDSHIP DANCE

*Some friends don't help,*
*but a true friend is closer*
*than your own family.*
PROVERBS 18:24 CEV

At this point in my life, I have all the horses I need. I say this so often that it is now a running joke between my husband and me. Dan reminded me of it recently when I added two more horses to the herd since the last time I uttered those words.

I suppose I can justify it by saying that they are horses I have previously boarded on my farm, so I just made the decision to make their stay more permanent. But I have all the horses I need for now. (And I emphasize the words *for now*!)

"I have all the friends I need." I've said that before too. But it took my friend Ashley to help me see that making new friends is pretty easy to do when we don't overthink the process.

I'm happy to say I have more quality friends than I've ever had in my

> Making new friends is pretty easy to do when we don't overthink the process.

life since I've fallen in love with Jesus. I view almost everyone as a potential friend, and I'm so excited to know that in my hope-filled future there will be an entire heaven and new earth filled with even more friends!

Back when I was just a little more foolish than I am now—and before I got back into horses—I thought it would be a good idea to start pursuing a tap dancing dream that I've secretly had. It sounded adventurous, and maybe I'd end up being the next Ginger Rogers. The trouble was my kids were toddlers at the time. I started attending classes at night, but it didn't take me long to realize that I did not have the time or the energy to leave my house after a day of chasing kids. I noticed that all the women in my class were empty nesters, some of them widows. So I got it—this was probably not a good time in my life to pursue tap dancing. My life was not going at a retiree's pace.

My tapping dreams were eventually whittled down to a private lesson one day a week at a health club after I would drop off my son at preschool.

As I rounded the corner at the top of the health club stairs toward the studio where my tap dance teacher was waiting, I heard a voice speaking to me from the direction of some free weights. What followed was one of the strangest exchanges I have had with a person who would later become one of my dearest confidantes.

"Do you have kids at the Christian school?"

"Who me?" I said, pointing at myself. "Um, yeah."

"What's your name?"

"Cara."

"I'm Ashley. Do you work out here?"

"Not really."

"What are you doing here then?"

"Tap dancing." My confession came with an awkward pause. "Uh, would you like to tap dance with me?"

"Yes."

And that was how I became friends with Ashley. Later, I discovered she is just as introverted as I am, and (at the time) she was also a babe still on spiritual milk in the Christian faith. It's so strange that only God could orchestrate an encounter so fabulously. Ashley is now one of my fiercest, most loyal battle buddies, and every so often we will recall that day when we had an encounter like it was right out of the pages of a guidebook for childhood friendship making.

We adults often gravitate to what's most comfortable, so we are happy to stick with the same people in our lives whom we made relationships with in our past. That's why kids are so fascinating to me. All they need is another human for them to find common ground, and suddenly they are making up a new playground game with a familiar stranger.

Ashley opened my eyes to see that I have an entire family of brothers and sisters in Christ. I just need to have the courage to approach situations with a more childlike perspective.

> We adults often gravitate to what's most comfortable, so we are happy to stick with the same people in our lives whom we made relationships with in our past.

My mind immediately flashed back to my first tap class. I decided not to be discouraged by the generational differences I saw, but instead to focus more on what makes us similar. And know what? Looking back, I realized that my class was actually full of women who shared the same secret desire to be the next Ginger Rogers.

Making friends is easy and fun. That's the attitude that motivated me to join a Bible study group with ladies who were twice my age. It has been one of my best faith-building experiences as I watch these gals run their Christian races. I am so glad that I didn't let age get in the way of all the things we have in common. And since becoming friends with them, I was a more effective witness the day I visited (and spoke at) my grandma's assisted-living home. And it runs both ways. I've also been able to help older friends see that generations even younger than me are not beyond their evangelistic reach.

Standing in one place among a group of the same people is not that difficult. It's comfortable. But the thing about comfort is, it's not that motivating. You can never have enough Christian friends, because they grow your faith and motivate you to care more about the people around you. Without realizing it, you will start to focus on all the things you have in common instead of focusing on all the things you don't.

So I can't make enough friends, and, well, I don't need any more horses!

Lord, thank You for giving me true friends. I'm jumping for joy that I will make many more friends in heaven. Help me to be the kind of friend who isn't afraid to share my eternal hope. Amen.

# CONCLUSION

## *Go, Love . . . and Grow God's Family*

From Genesis to Revelation, the Bible makes it clear how God feels about us: our lives are precious to Him. "So God created mankind in his own image, in the image of God he created them; male and female he created them" (Genesis 1:27). And in the Lord's eyes, we're much more than nameless faces in a sea of humanity. He loves us as individuals whom He knows intimately. We are the very workmanship of God (Ephesians 2:10); knit together in our mother's womb, fearfully and wonderfully made (Psalm 139:13–14). Incredibly, the Bible tells us that the very hairs of our head are all numbered by the Lord—that's how precious we are to Him (Luke 12:7).

Most of all, God doesn't want anyone to perish. He has called every believer to "go" and love others into His kingdom:

> I have been given all authority in heaven and on earth! Go to the people of all nations and make them my disciples. Baptize them in the name of the Father, the Son, and the Holy Spirit, and teach them to do every-thing I have told you. I will be with you always, even until the end of the world. (Matthew 28:18–20 CEV)

I've filled these pages with scriptures and inspiring stories that I pray will encourage you to share a liberating truth: God is crazy in love with us. His passion heals and transforms and is meant to "go to the people of all nations."

As you engage with God—and as Christ's love begins to surge through you—I hope you'll discover the miraculous: it overflows and touches others. Our Savior's love is much too great to be contained in a single human heart. It must be lived out and multiplied! "May the Lord make your love increase and overflow for each other and for everyone else, just as ours does for you" (1 Thessalonians 3:12).

Here's what I believe and what I hope you've caught in these pages: ordinary, everyday people can be a reflection of Christ and share His passion in extraordinary ways, not only through words but through actions. This is how the gospel penetrated the world during the first century: self-denying, Spirit-empowered disciples of Jesus invested in others and multiplied God's kingdom. Followers of Jesus went fishing for men, loving and serving in Christ's name—making other disciples. With each connection, they launched the journey of disciple-making, what Christian scholar Eugene H. Peterson referred to as "a long obedience in the same direction." It happens one connection at a time . . . and it sets in motion God's amazing kingdom-building math: disciples go, love, serve, and invest . . . which compels new disciples to go, love, serve, and invest . . . and so on.

...................................................................................

Lord Jesus, Your will be done on earth as it is in heaven. Amen.

# NOTES

## INTRODUCTION

1. Thomas Frey, "Future of Healthcare," July 27, 2016, futuristspeaker.com.

## CHAPTER 9: IF THE HAT FITS

1. Blair Parke, "Who Said 'Comparison Is the Thief of Joy' and How Is It Represented in the Bible?" Bible Study Tools, April 2, 2019, https://www.biblestudytools.com/bible-study/topical-studies/who-said-comparison-is-the-thief-of-joy.html.

## CHAPTER 13: CALVES IN JACKETS

1. Biography, "Jeffrey Dahmer: The Monster Within," TV documentary directed by Bill Harris, first aired June 3, 1996, on A&E, Tower Productions.
2. "Jeffrey Dahmer," directed by Bill Harris.

## CHAPTER 14: GOD CAN FIX A CRAZY LIFE

1. Anonymous source. Quote drawn from interview conducted by Michael Ross, August 10, 2004.

## CHAPTER 21: JUST LEAVE THE LIGHT ON

1. Max Lucado, *God's Promises for You* (Nashville: Thomas Nelson, 2006), 171.

## CHAPTER 25: HELL FOR COWS

1. C. S. Lewis, *The Problem of Pain* (New York: Macmillan, 1962), 127.

## CHAPTER 26: SWAPPING STORIES: MINE, YOURS, GOD'S

1. *Webster's New World Dictionary*, 2nd college ed. (New York: The World Publishing Company, 1976), s.v. "parable."
2. Josh Mulvihill, "When Do Americans Become Christians?" Gospel Shaped Family, August 13, 2018, https://www.gospelshapedfamily.com/discipleship/when-do-americans-become-christians/.

## CHAPTER 33: SALT YOUR CONVERSATIONS

1. Krishona Martinson, "Using Slow Feed Hay Nets," University of Minnesota Extension, 2018, https://extension.umn.edu/horse-nutrition/using-slow-feed-hay-nets.
2. "What Does It Mean That Believers Are to Be Salt and Light (Matthew 5:13-16)?" gotquestions.com, 2020, https://www.gotquestions.org/salt-and-light.html.

## CHAPTER 35: FRIEND OF SINNERS

1. Jonathan Parnell, "Three Tips on Being a Friend of Sinners," Desiring God, March 22, 2014, https://www.desiringgod.org/articles/three-tips-on-being-a-friend-of-sinners.
2. Parnell, "Three Tips."

## CHAPTER 38: TWO STEPS FORWARD, ONE STEP BACK

1. Michelle DeRusha, a wife, mother, and writer in Lincoln, Nebraska, contributed to this devotional entry. A portion of her story first appeared in Arnie Cole and Michael Ross, *Tempted, Tested, True: A Proven Path to Overcoming Soul-Robbing Choices* (Bloomington, MN: Bethany House, 2013) and is used with permission of the authors.

# ABOUT
# THE AUTHOR

C ara Whitney grew up on a cattle farm in northern Wisconsin. After spending a decade as a radio personality in markets that included Las Vegas, she found herself in search of that simpler life everyone talks about. She soon discovered there is no such thing as a simple life, but instead your best-lived life is one that includes a relationship with Jesus Christ. Cara lives with her husband and two kids on a horse farm in Nebraska.

# The Perfect Way
## *for Horse Lovers*
## TO START THE DAY

Explore the timeless wisdom of God's Word through this beautiful horse devotional, *Unbridled Faith: 100 Devotions from the Horse Farm*. Horses nuzzle their way into our hearts and have a way of teaching us a lot about ourselves, about life, and even about God. Just ask horse enthusiast Cara Whitney, wife of comedian and actor Dan Whitney (aka Larry the Cable Guy).

Foreword *by* Dan Whitney,
"Larry the Cable Guy"

UNBRIDLED FAITH
*100 Devotions
from the Horse Farm*

*Available everywhere books are sold*

# 1

# Welcome to the Barn Party

*"Rejoice with me; I have found my lost sheep."*
Luke 15:6

My funny horse is the life of the barn party. His name is Sven, but I call him Fat Benny. He can gain five pounds just by looking at grass (just like my husband with a cheeseburger). He is very vocal, so if he sees me, he will whinny. But as big as he is, his whinny is very wimpy. Fat Benny knows he's fat, so if he wants something on the other side of the fence, he lays on the fence until it collapses and just rolls over the top of it. Benny's antics give joy to everyone at the barn.

Whether it's through your animals, kids, or friends, if you're like me, you find joy in a lot of different ways. However, if you and I want to share the joy of heaven, we need to find our greatest joy in salvation. Jesus told us that there will be "more rejoicing in heaven over one sinner who repents than over ninety-nine righteous persons who do not need to repent" (Luke 15:7).

Our upside-down culture prizes fast cars, expensive clothes, fleeting fame, and shallow relationships over eternal blessings. But as citizens of the kingdom of God, we should put our salvation—and that of those around us—at the top of our lists of things that bring us joy. Think of it: the angels rejoice when one of God's human creations comes to faith in

Him. If you have accepted Jesus as your Savior, the heavenly beings celebrated when you confessed Him as Lord.

There will be a party in heaven for you! Now, doesn't that make you want to kick up *your* heels?

........................................................................................................

*Lord, thank You for the gift of salvation—and the great celebration that awaits Your followers in heaven, amen.*

# 2

## IT'S OKAY TO NOT BE OKAY

*"I no longer call you servants, because a servant does not know his master's business. Instead, I have called you friends."*
JOHN 15:15

Horses are amazing animals. When I feel sad or depressed, my horses seem to sense my pain. They turn their ears toward me and even lean into me. In those moments, they aren't just sweet creatures to ride, train, and enjoy; instead, they are my friends.

Still, even if we're surrounded by comforting friends, at some time in our lives, we will be hit with pain so excruciating we will wonder if there is any point in going on. Whether it's a financial crisis, a health catastrophe, or a relationship implosion, our very souls will cry out, "This is too much! I can't live through this!"

Yet with God, we don't have to pretend everything is okay. He longs to be the "friend who sticks closer than a brother" (Proverbs 18:24). He created us, so He knows us better than we know ourselves. We can be honest and real with Him. And His power can help us endure tough seasons. We just have to be humble enough to admit we need Him. You are not big enough to handle life on your own. Run into the arms of a heavenly Father who loves you and weeps with you. Trust Him to be the most loyal, best friend you've ever had.

*Lord, thank You for being not only my creator, sustainer, and savior, but also my friend, amen.*

# Calling all fillies, colts, and ponies!

*Unbridled Faith Devotions for Young Readers* by Cara Whitney takes your child into the country with stunning photographs of horses paired with devotions that celebrate the spiritual truths these majestic animals teach us.

unbridled faith

DEVOTIONS *for* YOUNG READERS

CARA WHITNEY

# NOTES

# NOTES